Judaism in the American Humanities

BROWN UNIVERSITY
BROWN JUDAIC STUDIES
Edited by
Jacob Neusner
Wendell S. Dietrich, Ernest S. Frerichs,
Sumner B. Twiss, Alan Zuckerman

Board of Editors

David Altshuler, George Washington University
David R. Blumenthal, Emory University
Baruch M. Bokser, University of California, Berkeley
Joel Gereboff, Arizona State University
David Goldenberg, Dropsie University
Robert Goldenberg, State University of New York, Stony Brook
David Goodblatt, Haifa University
William Scott Green, University of Rochester
Peter Haas, Vanderbilt University
Martin Jaffee, University of Virginia
Shamai Kanter, Temple Beth El, Rochester, New York
Jack L. Lightstone, Concordia University
Irving Mandelbaum, University of Texas
Alan Mintz, University of Maryland
Alan J. Peck, Tulane University
Gary G. Porton, University of Illinois
Marc L. Raphael, Ohio State University
Richard S. Sarason, Hebrew Union College-Jewish Institute of Religion
Tzvee Zahavy, University of Minnesota

Editorial Committee:

Roger Brooks
Louis Newman

Number 28
JUDAISM IN THE AMERICAN HUMANITIES

Essays and Reflections

by Jacob Neusner

JUDAISM IN THE AMERICAN HUMANITIES
Essays and Reflections

by
Jacob Neusner

Scholars Press

Distributed by
SCHOLARS PRESS
101 Salem Street
Chico, California 95926

JUDAISM IN THE AMERICAN HUMANITIES

Essays and Reflections

by

Jacob Neusner

Copyright © 1981
Brown University

Library of Congress Cataloging in Publication Data

Neusner, Jacob, 1932–
  Judaism in the American humanities.

  (Brown Judaic studies ; no. 28)
  Includes index.
  1. Judaism--Study and teaching (Higher)--United
States--Addresses, essays, lectures. 2. Jews--
History--Study and teaching (Higher)--United States--
Addresses, essays, lectures. 3. Judaism--History--
Talmudic period, 10-425--Historiography--Addresses,
essays, lectures. I. Title. II. Series.
BM75.N48   909'.04924   81-1798
ISBN 0-89130-480-0   AACR2

Printed in the United States of America
1 2 3 4 5 6
Edwards Brothers, Inc.
Ann Arbor, Michigan 48106

To
Emanuel Rackman
and
Bar Ilan University

TABLE OF CONTENTS

Preface ix
Acknowledgments xvii

Part I
REFLECTIONS OF A COUNCILLOR

1 Defining the Humanities: Clearing Away Some Debris 3
2 Defining the Humanities: From Many, One? 13
3 Stranger at Home: Toward a Theory of the Humanistic Study of Religion 23
4 NEH Occasions: Who Chooses? 39
5 NEH Occasions: Open Meetings 45
6 NEH Occasions: The Humanities, Public Policy, and Organized Jewry 49

Part II
HUMANISTIC APPROACHES TO TEACHING ABOUT JUDAISM

7 Contexts and Constituencies: The Diverse Responsibilities of Higher Jewish Learning 55
8 Contexts and Curricula: Introducing Judaism in the Humanities. The First Course and its Problems 67
9 Contexts and Classrooms: Modes of Academic Advocacy. The Case of Judaism 83

Part III
HUMANISTIC APPROACHES TO THE STUDY OF JUDAISM
Theory and Practice

10 Toward a Theory of Comparison: Alike and Not Alike. A Grid for Comparison and Differentiation 91
11 Toward a Theory of Category-Formation: Shaping Useful Categories. The Problem of "Judaism," "Christianity," and "Hellenism" 101
12 Toward a Theory of Talmudic "Lives": The Present State of Rabbinic Biography 107
13 Some Consequences of Theory: Religion and Society in Ancient Judaism with Special Reference to the Second and Third Centuries 113

Part IV
EPILOGUE

14 Judaic Studies as the Humanities of the Jewish Heritage   139

Appendix
    Clearing Away Some More Debris: Defining the Humanities
        Harold Cannon
        National Endowment for the Humanities   151

Index to Biblical and Talmudic References   155

General Index   157

PREFACE

These essays and reflections take up two matters linked through a context and experience unique to this writer, first, the encompassing encounter with the American humanities through labor of review and oversight within the principal federal program for humanistic learning and expression; second, the labor of teaching about and scholarship in Judaism within the study of religions. If this effort to discuss in a single way and framework two quite distinct topics turns out to attain a single plane of discourse, there is a reason. It is because the academic study of religions in general, and of Judaism in particular, forms a significant component of the American humanities today, and because the insights and intellectual attainments of the American humanities indeed shape the national purpose and contribute richly to the public interest. So I have tried to learn from encounters with public programs in the humanities lessons for the shaping of the Judaic sector of the humanities, on the one side, and to contribute something out of that Judaic tradition of humanistic learning and expression in discussions of the public policy and interest in the humanities, on the other.

At the outset let me say what I think we do in laboring at humanistic learning and what we propose to express in humanistic expression.

In the humanities we focus upon one aspect of our being, our imagination and sensibility, our capacity to appreciate and accordingly to respond to the being of humanity. What we teach in the humanities, that thing which sets us apart, is a work of imagination. It is an artifact of sensibility capable of both exemplifying and of allowing access to the unmeasured capacities of humanity to be: to laugh and cry, to feel pain and joy, to hope and endure, so to be as to surpass what we are. The intellect is common to us all. The use of intellect for the discovery of what we may become is the work of humanistic study. For what humanists study is what some have been and done which is worthy of attention and even emulation. When we use our minds to explore the potentialities of imagination, we come to history, philosophy, and literature. For these disciplines explore the great works of imagination and passion (not alone of intellect) and allow us to experience, in the deeds and vision of other men and women, those hitherto unimagined thoughts, unseen visions, unheard sounds, and unplumbed depths of mature emotion, by which we may measure and shape our own capacity and so transcend our small and limited selves.

There is no common core of humanistic facts which everyone everywhere must know and which we in particular teach. Nor is there a distinctive grace of intellect which is ours alone. All we have to offer is a particular access: to those moments in history of significant humanness; to those powerful minds in philosophy of transcendent self-awareness; to those sensibilities in literature, and to those anguished, searching hearts in religions, in which we may perceive not what we are but what we too can be. This is another kind of classicism: the conviction, which is the value we espouse and profess, that greatness inheres in humanity; that it is worthwhile being human. By the exercise of catholic taste and critical judgment we may make choices among works of human greatness of mind and emotion. Through the selection of what our frail judgment tells us transcends ourselves and surpasses our former expectation, we too may know and therefore be more than what we know we are. In the humanities we teach by showing what humanity has been, has made, and has thought. This is how people have become more than what they are, and what students, the future and the hope, can feel and do and be and think. Some men and women have known how passionately to care and dream. These we teach: the creations of their caring and their passion.

If the humanities address issues of all times, in this modest book of essays I speak of acutely contemporary matters and mean to stimulate discussion relevant to this country at this hour. Specifically, I offer essays and reflections important to the humanities in this country. These take shape within that small corner of humanistic teaching and learning framed by the study of Judaism within the study of religions. These papers therefore are meant to be occasional, to serve a particular context. While, as I said, the setting is particular to me, I have tried to frame issues for discussion in broad and wide-ranging settings. For if the study of Judaism within the humanities leads to interesting insight, it is insight to be shared among those who study both other religions and other humanistic creations entirely. The particular then is made to illuminate the general, and the mode of thought is to deem the particular to be exemplary. Each statement about the study of Judaism is meant to be preceded by an e.g., that is, to serve as an example of some point common to the humanities. The reason is that it is relevant to the analysis and interpretation of the human condition. I hope that these papers will be read and found timely by humanists in diverse

PREFACE

circumstances of humanistic learning and expression, in government as much as in universities, in schools as much as in the academy, in the study as much as in the classroom. I have tried to frame the issues confronting me in particular in terms accessible and engaging for humanists, both in government and in universities, in general.

The source of the effort and ambition is obvious to me. From the time that President Carter appointed me as Member of the National Council on the Humanities, board of oversight and review of the National Endowment for the Humanities, I have tried to learn the lessons imparted by this, for me, extraordinary context.

Two issues, in particular, engaged my attention. First, I wanted to know what we mean by "the humanities," and why there should be a public program aimed at the nurture and dissemination of humanistic learning and expression. Second, I wished to learn how the humanities might reshape my understanding of my own field of study, so that I might become a better teacher and scholar.

All of the papers in this book were occasioned or shaped by my encounter with the National Endowment for the Humanities. Those in the first part take up concrete and current issues of definition and policy. Those in the second and the third parts do not relate in so obvious a way to the present, public position in which I serve. But, in fact, the questions raised and viewpoints expressed in them come to me out of the applications I have read and discussions I have followed within the Endowment and on the Council.

These are reports, then, about things I have learned, issues I have faced, in a world alien to the experience of most people apt to read this book. I write letters, I suppose, from a distant city, telling people what I think they may want to know about a place they are not likely to enter, a city of politics about the human spirit, a world of faith shared by a very few. These letters from a faraway place and alien condition may prove worth reading only if the insight and experience in the end are to be shared, reshaped into terms accessible and important beyond the bounds within which they are written. What the humanities do is teach us to turn what is private into something suggestive and evocative, to transform the particular into an instance of the general. That is a fair criterion for success. Whether or not in these papers I do succeed is not for me to say. But I also do not mean to apologize for them.

Let me now explain the purpose and sequence of the papers and introduce them.

The book is in three parts, beginning with the most general and readily accessible, ending with the most particular, but I hope, available, in its issues and results. The first part of the book takes up issues of theory and practice in public programs in the humanities, with the opening two papers concerned with theory, the next three with concrete and practical issues. The second and third parts of the book follow this same pattern of treating issues first of theory, then of practice. The second part addresses humanistic approaches to teaching about Judaism, with one theoretical paper on context and constituencies of the Jewish humanities, and two practical ones on shaping the curriculum and teachers' conceptions of the classroom, respectively. The third part, along these same lines, briefly takes up three issues of theory, and ends with a substantive account of a particular problem, an account informed by, and consequent upon, the problems of theory treated in the preceding papers.

Part I: The simple issue in Chapters One, Two and Three is how we define the humanities. I defend the insistence that an ongoing exercise of definition is critical to the humanities, not only to prevent clichés and jargon from taking over our powers of speech and thought about what we do. It also serves to explain to ourselves what contribution, if any, humanists have to make to the common good and how they serve the public interest.

For me the challenge of engagement with the National Council on the Humanities and the National Endowment for the Humanities has been to master the language and thought of colleagues in the federal humanities so as to make sense of what we do even in the chaos of concrete decision-making. Out of the decisions we make comes a clear perception of the policy, the theory, we follow in making decisions. But that is only if we look critically and objectively at what we have done, and ask how and whether it makes a difference. It is that self-critical exercise which is undertaken in the exercises of clarification presented at the outset. These papers were written in the opening two years of my membership on the Council, 1978–1980. If occasion arises, I hope to carry forward what is, in fact, a sequential and continuous discourse. The question raised in Chapter One is addressed in Chapters Two and Three. The next three papers are practical. They treat concrete issues confronting the Endowment. I keep them appropriately brief, since they respond to occasions and transient issues. They are meant to exemplify one mode of discourse. They attempt to explore one way of thinking about humanistic learning and expression within the framework of public life.

Part II: Chapters Seven, Eight, and Nine deal with the questions, who teaches what to whom, why and where? These matters define the character of humanistic learning, in ways in which they do not govern

PREFACE

the character of scientific studies. It is in the nature of the humanities that who teaches the subject, in what context, for what purpose, and within what frame of reference, will shape humanistic learning. The humanities are particular to those who study them. That is quite natural, for the subject who is taught, the student, in the present context defines the subject which is taught, the course. The consequences of that fact are worked out within the exemplification offered by the study of Judaism.

In the chapter on constituencies, I sharply distinguish among a number of contexts in which Judaism is studied and indicate what makes the humanistic context fructifying and stimulating. Consequences for the institutional organization of the Jewish humanities are spelled out. The setting—efforts to revive a dying school—is unhappily apt. In the discussion of the introductory course I try to explain what it means, so to speak, "to meet an educational payroll." I find myself impatient with people rich in opinions about how and what we should teach, but poor in concrete experience, poorer still in the capacity for self-criticism and scholarship. In the range of suggestions of how a single educational task in the humanities is done, namely, the work of introducing the religion of Judaism to students in university classrooms, the complexity of the problem is indicated.

The third paper once more stresses the discontinuity between the humanistic frame of discourse and that separate, distinct, and (at least) equally important frame of discourse constructed by the institutions of the living faith. In this context, they are community, synagogue, religious school; in others, churches of various sorts and their seminaries and schools. The reasons for the discontinuity must then be spelled out. No invidious comparisons are intended (though some may be drawn). Here too the concrete issues of teaching a specific subject to living and breathing students—as distinct from the theoretical issues about which people argue—are again framed in terms of Judaism, but the intent is to speak about a broad range of educational settings.

Part III: The last four chapters once more attempt to illustrate the character of humanistic learning, in the framework of the study of religions. This is worked out through a sustained account of problems of the humanistic description and interpretation of the Judaic religious tradition and its social and historical character. Since the study of religion invariably involves the comparison of religions, the opening paper takes up the issue of how comparisons are effected and for what purpose. This issue is a far more complex one than I am able to suggest, because it involves profound philosophical issues. But there is no reason to desist from discussion merely because one reasons from a particular set of tasks of comparison to a general theory of comparison.

The eleventh and twelfth papers run parallel to the fourth, fifth and sixth. That is, they are brief, and each is written about a single, severely limited issue. The former simply raises the question of how, in any event, we are able to speak about "Judaism" or "Christianity," since these categories tend to distort the data organized within them. This issue runs parallel to that of Chapter Two, on "the humanities." The latter equally simply points out that, since we do not really have "lives" of the ancient rabbis, we have to rethink the purposes for which study of the materials produced by those rabbis may be asked to serve.

Chapter 13 is meant to exemplify aspects of the three which go before. It takes up a question of broad interest, the relationship of religious ideas to the social group that holds them. This inevitably involves an exercise in comparison, for the very formation of the question, deriving as it does from the writings of Max Weber, depends upon a theory of comparison and a program for comparative studies. It further avoids the organizing category, "Judaism," and instead defines the frame of reference in terms more adequate to the data under discussion. Finally, it treats the evidence in a way appropriate to the character of the evidence, that is to say, not as reports of one time historical events, things which were said or done on some one day, but rather, as ongoing statements of the enduring character of imagination and sensibility, general comments on the world effected through specific judgments on small things.

My hope, finally, is that this substantive paper will serve to exemplify a mode of discourse, within the study of Judaism, appropriate to humanistic learning and relevant, in its own way, to issues of public policy. In asking about how a small group of intellectuals reshaped a vision of society in response to disaster and defeat surely I take up a world analogous to that of our own country at this time. For one task confronting humanists in particular is to explore the dark corners of a society which has suffered defeat and seeks renewal, a nation calling for renaissance of the national will and purpose through the resources of its own spirit. This is precisely what I take to be the achievement of the small and provincial rabbis of the Land of Israel in the later first and second centuries, who produced Judaism as we know it. In explaining how and what they were thinking, and the way in which the attainments of mind responded to the realm in which they did their work of mind, I mean to show the power and promise of humanistic learning and expression in all ages and circumstances—the power of the human mind to take hold of the human condition and reform and reshape both intellect and heart.

PREFACE

With its focus upon the definition of the humanities and the place of the study of Judaism without the humanities, this book is a companion to a now completed trilogy: *The Academic Study of Judaism* (N.Y.: Ktav, 1975), *The Academic Study of Judaism* (Second Series) (N.Y.: Ktav, 1977), and *The Academic Study of Judaism* (Third Series): *Three Contexts of Jewish Learning* (N.Y.: Ktav, 1980). Those groups of essays systematically take up the much narrower issue of defining Judaic studies within the context of a university and of discovering for sustained discussion the fresh issues confronting Judaic learning presented by that unprecedented setting. The papers here, by contrast, treat questions of more encompassing interest and concern.

This book is complete on the eve of yet another trip to address a conference at an Israeli university: this one is to Bar Ilan University for a conference on "Jewish studies as the humanities of the Jewish heritage." In many ways the thirteenth and the fourteenth papers complement one another. The former speaks of the human intellect in the face of calamity; the latter, of the human intellect in the confrontation with crisis and opportunity. In the thirteenth chapter I try to explain how the intellectuals invented a world to replace a lost age. In the fourteenth I propose to suggest how intellectuals may confront the critical issues of their own day, doing so not in politics but wholly within the framework of their own rigorous disciplines of the mind. My argument is that the study of religions as defined within the humanities not only raises central issues for the interpretation of culture, society, and history, but it also bears within itself the power to overcome contemporary crises of mind and imagination in culture and society. In a country such as the State of Israel, in which religions flourish but are not studied within the humanities, I try to explain why the humanistic study of religions may lead to understanding and make for peace. I cannot think of a more striking demonstration of what is to be learned from the study of Judaism within the American humanities, nor of a more appropriate dedication for these papers.

Through this dedication I express my thanks to President Rackman and to his colleagues at Bar Ilan University for the honor of their invitation and for the thoughtful reception accorded to this paper. I thank them also for that hospitality for which colleagues in the State of Israel may be justly famous.

Jacob Neusner

Providence, Rhode Island
27 Adar II 5741
April 2, 1981

ACKNOWLEDGMENTS

The papers in this book originated as follows:

"Defining the Humanities. I. Clearing Away Some Debris," address at Augustana College, Rock Island, Illinois, on March 27, 1979. Originally printed in my *The Academic Study of Judaism. Essays and Reflections* (Third Series): *Three Contexts of Jewish Learning* (N.Y.: Ktav, 1980), pp. 36-47.

"Defining the Humanities. II. From Many, One?," address at the annual dinner, Rhode Island Alpha of Phi Beta Kappa, at Brown University, on March 24, 1980. Previously unpublished.

"Stranger at Home," originally printed in *The Academic Study of Judaism* (Third Series), pp. 16-35.

"Who decides?," previously unpublished.

"Open Discussion," in *Humanities Report* 2, 7, 1979, No. 19, pp. 2-3.

"The Humanities, Public Policy, and Organized Jewry," address at the joint meeting of the National Endowment for the Humanities and the Council of Jewish Federations, in Washington, D.C., on May 12, 1980, on the Humanities and the Jewish community. Previously unpublished.

"Contexts and Constituencies. The Diverse Responsibilities of Higher Jewish Learning," address at Dropsie University, Philadelphia, on October 8, 1980. Previously unpublished.

"Contexts and Curricula" as "Introducing Judaism in the University: The First Course and Its Problems," *Journal of Reform Judaism* 26, 3, 1979, pp. 35-54.

"Modes of Academic Advocacy: The Case of Judaism," in the *Alfred Jospe Festschrift* (N.Y.: Ktav, 1980), pp. 99-104.

"Alike and Not Alike: A Grid for Comparison and Differentiation," previously unpublished.

"Shaping Useful Categories: The Problem of 'Christianity,' 'Judaism,' and 'Hellenism,'" previously unpublished.

"The Present State of Rabbinic Biography," in *Homage à George Vajda* (Louvain: 1980), pp. 85–91.

"Religion and Society in Ancient Judaism," The Sacks Lecture at Oxford University on May 12, 1981. Previously unpublished.

"Jewish Studies as the Humanities of the Jewish Heritage," at Bar Ilan University on April 2, 1981. Previously unpublished.

Part I
Reflections of a Councillor

CHAPTER 1

Defining the Humanities: Clearing Away Some Debris

The power of the humanities, we generally suppose, is their access to the common imagination.[1] That is, we all are human. We know the facts of humanities, so the humanities are ours. The pathos of the humanities is their incapacity to make distinctions and find definition. So *what* we all know we do not know. Since we all are human, why are your facts more factual than mine? And why is your opinion more apt to be sound than mine? In fact this chronic crisis of definition, which has been upon us for so long, may be a stimulus to health. But it is not a sign of health. For if we do not know what we think we are doing when we teach, study, or practice something we designate as "humanistic," we are not going to know, either, good from bad. Without a clear picture of what we want to achieve, we shall not be able to exercise taste and judgment. We are left to say, "I think . . . , you think. . . ."

The absence of suitable definitions for exposition and argument—I do not ask for something so great as a consensus among humanists—yields not silence, but empty speech. There is recourse to convenience—language, for example, to catalogues. Indeed, the humanities are one of the few areas of abstract thought and culture in which the federal government has given us a legislative definition. If I may quote *Public Law 209, 89th Congress, as amended through October 8, 1976*, that is, the basic legislation which is called the *National Foundation on the Arts and the Humanities Act of 1965*,[2] I find two sorts of definitions. In the nature of things, neither is going to be wholly satisfactory. But if we may exercise our imagination and place ourselves in the offices of the people who formulated the law, we shall see how they solved their problem—or evaded it and bequeathed it to us.

---

[1] Address at Augustana College, Rock Island, Illinois, March 27, 1979.
[2] As legislation goes, the writing of this act must be regarded as unusually skillful and careful. Some of the passages quoted below are far more than routine rhetoric. I also happen to believe that, in substance, this act must be regarded as one of the great pieces of legislature in our day.

Let me begin with "definitions." The term humanities is defined in the following way (*Sec. 3, 20 U.S.C. 952*):

> As used in this Act, the term humanities includes, but is not limited to, the study of the following: language, both modern and classical; linguistics; literature; history; jurisprudence; philosophy; archaeology; comparative religion; ethics; the history, criticism, theory, and practice of the arts; those aspects of the social sciences which have humanistic content and employ humanistic methods; and the study and application of the humanities to the human environment with particular attention to the relevance of the humanities to the current conditions of national life.

Now, as Richard Lyman of The Rockefeller Foundation has already pointed out ("Keynote Address of the 1978 National Meeting of State Humanities Programs," reprinted in *Federation Reports*, II, 4, 1978), what the "Congressional definition" supplies is in fact a catalogue. This definition, as he says, "Winds up in a burst of question-begging: it is not clear just how we'll recognize 'those aspects of the social sciences which have humanistic content and employ humanistic methods' if we have no guidance as to what 'humanistic' means beyond a list of academic disciplines."

This observation of President Lyman runs very deep. For defining the humanities by reference to those disciplines which fall into the division of the humanities on the surface begs the question of definition.[3] It generates a fantasy: "We all know what we're talking about." This fantastic notion frees us of the obligation to define our terms, to specify the purpose of our conversation. This same attitude of mind expresses itself in the ubiquitous surrender to exemplification: if we give enough examples of what we imagine we mean, we shall discover what it is that we mean. That simply does not serve.

In reports to the Council and to Congress, the tendency of National Endowment for the Humanities' leaders—people of exceptional intellect and fine judgment—will commonly give lists of things we have done and are doing with public funds: a dictionary here, a youth project there. This is a resort to the poetry of symbolism. The dictionary is supposed to symbolize all the dictionaries, the youth project, all the humanistic things young people do. We become prisoners of our symbol. We begin to think that humanistic work is the making of dictionaries or the conduct of oral histories by high school students. The symbol does not evoke. It defines. And those questions of public policy before the Council and before Congress and its committees tend then not to be discussed at all. So the making of

---

[3]At the end I shall offer something very like what I criticize at this point, but for different reasons and with a different purpose.

CLEARING AWAY DEBRIS 5

catalogues which begins in our original legislation evades a problem and complicates it at the same time.[4]

Before turning to the other exercise in definition contained in the original legislation, I want to dwell on the limitations of the "Congressional definition." What it says, first of all, is something it cannot possibly mean. This is that the term humanities refers to the *study* of a given subject, with remarkably slight interest in the *practice* or *application* of that subject. We have, after all, a mere list of subjects. It is only at the end that we are told we refer to "the study and application of the humanities to the human environment. . . ." Now there is an interesting gap here. The subjects of languages, history, comparative religion, and the like are humanistic, though what is humanistic about them is not specified. Only when we speak of the humanities in general, when we leave the specificities of the list of suitable subjects, do we refer to the matter of "application." Then we speak of "attention to the relevance of the humanities to the current conditions of national life." This I take to mean the application of the humanities or the practice of the humanities, and not merely the *study* of them.

To put matters otherwise: when I practice my academic specialty which is the study of history of religions, I fall into one of the categories of the humanities. But it is only that I fall within that larger category of *humanist* when I study and apply the humanities, now no longer my *specific* thing. What is missing, clearly, is a notion of what is meant by the *applied humanities*. That is why emphasis is placed upon study, rather than upon humanistic expression or humanistic practice.[5]

Let me now express the three elements of this part of the problem simply. First, the making of a list of subjects which all together add up

---

[4]It should be noted that the presentation of the NEH budget to OMB and to Congress, by contrast, contains a remarkably clear and lucid account of the Endowment and its work. In fact there is no better way to grasp the whole of the NEH and its work than to read the FY 1980 budget, with its careful and completely accessible account of each program and division. So the NEH knows full well what it is doing. In its serious account of itself, the NEH in no way resorts to the evasion consisting of long lists of "examples" which in the end exemplify only our incapacity to overcome confusion. That is to say, the NEH knows full well what it is doing. That is so even though the public rhetoric now in hand does not facilitate the Endowment's showing how what it does accords with a generally accepted notion of what it is that humanities and humanists do in general. So the quest for definition encompasses the Endowment, but it is not the work solely or mainly of the Endowment.

[5]This is not the place in which to explore the notion of the *applied humanities*. But it has to be said that within both NEH and state programs in the humanities there is developing a corpus of experience on the social application of the humanities and the public practice of the humanities. In time I think we shall have much to teach the world about this notion.

to "the humanities" imposes a double identity on each of those subjects. As I just said, it tells me that when I study religions, I am doing something else as well, which is also studying humanities. When I study history, I am also studying humanities, so too with literature, jurisprudence, linguistics, and the like. But what is it that I am doing "once which is twice," so to speak? What is that *other* thing which I also am doing at the moment at which I study history or literature or religions or philosophy? This I do not know. Whether the list is long or short, I am not much helped by asking what all the items on the list have in common.

Second, the catalogue is remarkably vague about humanistic expression. It appears that it is all right to study poetry, but poets fall outside of the frame of reference. So far as poetry is not relevant to the current conditions of national life, that is, so far as the poet expresses something merely private, if also in a public way, it is not contained within the definition, even, of the applied humanities. There is an academic bias built into the making of lists, which speak of language, literature, history, philosophy, but not of writers, historians, philosophers, or poets (I omit all reference, now, to practitioners of religions, for obvious and valid reasons). Where, in other words, is there space for the one who does not study a humanistic field but who cultivates that field? In point of fact the vast portion of the resources of the National Endowment for the Humanities is devoted to humanistic *expression*—to people who propose to apply "the humanities" and to practice them. These proposals are sound and important. Given the range and breadth of the culture of this country, the applied humanities deserve all the support they receive, and more.[6] But within the stated catalogue we find a bias, which does not exist in fact, in favor of the learning, and not the doing, of these things.

Third, list-making smacks of academic politics. That is, they turn out to list those subjects or disciplines represented in the room on the day on which the list was made. The invisible hand always does its wondrous work. That, of course, is not fair to the seriousness of the people who wrote the legislation. But we do have a habit of seeing the world through the eyes of everyone we know—and of no one whom

---

[6]Once more I emphasize that our practices have now outrun our theoretical framework. That is why it is so difficult to know good from bad "applied humanities." We rely on the guidance of the critical intuitions of our program officers and panelists (speaking within the grant-making framework) or our communities and their instinctively sound judgments. When we resort to an instinct about what works and what does not work, it is time for much more serious discourse of a theoretical character than we have undertaken. This is typical of our country's culture: do first, then think about it.

we do not know, an easy and natural thing. The reason that definitions of a core-curriculum are so often suspect is the same. In the end they embody the claim that all of human culture may be stated within the consensus of the powerful professors of this or that discipline or aspect of culture. It may well be that a more comprehensive, suggestive, or supple definition is not to be attained. I am not sure any of us can have done better. But there is the suspicion, generated in the encounter with any such catalogue, that there either is too much or too little. The list is either too long, because it specifies so much as to eliminate what is not listed, or it is too short, because it leaves out things that lie, at present, beyond our imagination—or our circle of friends.

So the begging of the question to which President Lyman directs our attention is deep. It brings us to the suspicion that suitable exercises in definition yield only unsuitable definitions. What is rigorous, encompassing, and truly definitive may either be trite or vacuous. So we are left with a considerable and urgent task which may be, in the end, unattainable. If we cannot climb over the mountains, we may have to find the passes around them. But what a view we are going to miss!

Let me now call attention to yet a second exercise in definition, contained also within the original legislation of 1965, the Congressional declaration of purpose. What we have before us now is not a definition, but a statement of purpose. This, in its way, provides those criteria for good and bad which serve to point toward and define, just as precisely as a verbal formula, what we mean. Let me quote at some length language which I think is both evocative and careful:

> The Congress hereby finds and declares:
> (1) that the encouragement and support of national progress and scholarship in the humanities, while primarily a matter for private and local initiative, is also an appropriate matter of concern to the federal Government;
> (2) that a high civilization must not limit its efforts to science and technology alone, but must give full value and support to the other great branches of man's scholarly and cultural activity in order to achieve a better understanding of the past, a better analysis of the present, and a better view of the future;
> (3) that democracy demands wisdom and vision in its citizens and that it must therefore foster and support a form of education designed to make men masters of their technology and not its unthinking servant;
> (4) that it is necessary and appropriate for the federal Government to complement, assist, and add to programs for the advancement of the humanities and the arts by local, state, regional, and private agencies and their organizations;
> (5) that the practice of art and the study of the humanities requires constant dedication and devotion, and that, while no government can call a great artist or scholar into existence, it is necessary and appropriate for the federal government to help create and sustain not only a climate encouraging freedom of thoughts,

imagination, and inquiry, but also the material conditions facilitating the release of this creative talent;

(6) that the world leadership which has come to the United States cannot rest solely upon superior power, wealth, and technology, but must be solidly founded upon worldwide respect and admiration for the Nation's high qualities as a leader in the realms of ideas and of the spirit. . . .

Now what I think is important in these words is a different effort at stating what humanistic expression and learning are meant to mean. What the author provides is a social definition of what humanists do, whether they do it for love or for money, and what they are supposed to accomplish.

Humanists are meant to be people in search of understanding, people capable of analysis, and people with the power of vision to contemplate a future worth having. Obviously, we speak now of all of us, of a country which cares for wisdom and seeks understanding. What this definition does not do, of course, is to exclude. Just as the definition made up of a list of subjects fails because of what it does not include, so a set of purposes encompasses too much. The stated goals are sound. I should not want anyone to dismiss them merely because they are noble. But they do not tell us what a humanist is not. So they encompass altogether too many things to help us define what a humanist *is*.

The rest of the statement of purpose now falls into place. Point three—mastering technology—once more refers to purposes which are to be achieved by people who may not also be linguists, historians, philosophers, or comparative religionists. Whether or not great artists and great scholars may be called into being by an infusion of federal funds, or, even, public esteem and attention, the claim here is that great artists and great scholars win for our nation worldwide respect and admiration for our high qualities as a leader in the realm of ideas and of the spirit. This remains to be demonstrated.

We have dealt with the two most prominent and consequential definitions of the humanities available at this time, the statement of what humanities are, and the statement of what humanities are supposed to accomplish. While it is easy to criticize the people who make catalogues of our work in humanistic study and expression and expect those catalogues to do the unattempted work of definition, we now can see the reason. If you do not have more than facts, then at least give facts. Out there, there may be a mind able to make some sense and find some meaning in them. And, at least, "we all know" what the facts are.

That, alas, is not so. Our language raises its own complications, which are not of our own, or our Congress's, making. To these we have now to turn. The fundamental problem is that the word, *humanities*, sounds like, and is related to, other words: *humanitarian* and *humane*, for example. The result is that people assume *humanities* have something to do with being nice, on the personal side, or solving social problems, on the public side. As John H. Barcroft stated in a memo (January 26, 1972), "The Office of Education mounts programs which bring university resources to bear on practical community problems; the humanities means humane and humanitarian; therefore a humanities program aimed at the public must mean getting humanists to plan public housing or helping poor people." Barcroft further points out that humanities are compared to the arts and related to them. Therefore, he says, "an arts program is the Boston Symphony, *Waiting for Godot*, and an art exhibit; therefore a humanities program must be someone celebrating Beethoven, Beckett, and Braque." Barcroft's observations come right to the heart of the problem of public discourse. They therefore underline the urgency of the ongoing work of definition. That is why I turn to his memo for guidance on the way ahead.

Obviously, we are not going to attain in a day or in a speech that clarity of vision and consistency of purpose which we seek. Nor shall we find in other worlds and other cultures the definitions of what we do. Though we may admire the writings of humanistic definition and inquiry emerging from other English-speaking countries, and though there is much to learn from the thoughts of humanists and the modes of public organization and public expression of the humanities in Europe, Asia, Latin America, and Africa, in fact the problem is ours. The solution must come from our particular world. For we have a National Endowment for the Humanities and not a Canada Council or a Ministry of Culture (to name two modes of political organization employed elsewhere). We have not distinctive but unique institutions—the liberal arts B.A., the state commissions on the humanities, the popular and academic societies of humanistic expression and learning, at home and across the nation. Ours is a world of breathtaking diversity. Fundamental to our culture is respect for diversity amid the quest for commonality and unity. The problematic of definition here as in other critical areas of our national life is shaped by that profound respect. It is what makes our work difficult and what perhaps in the end will permit consensus only upon cliché. We cannot know. We have not begun the work.

To begin with, I think we have to ask what humanists appropriately may be asked to do, and what they cannot do. In this regard, Barcroft's memo yields yet another profound insight:

> The best way to be sure that you are not defining the humanities unrealistically or asking the humanist to do unrealistic and inappropriate things, is to have some academic humanists sitting with you as full participants as you plan and implement your [public] program [in the humanities]. There is another reason. It is possible to mount a public program in the humanities which causes the public to know that Aristotle and Locke existed and were both useful and thoughtful, and *not* to know that there are living people in the United States who spend their lives trying to deal with the same kinds of intellectual problems that Locke dealt with—and are also both useful and thoughtful. The object then is to be sure that the public comes to some better understanding and use of the 100,000 or so American academic humanists who are not dead and who need the support, understanding, and attention of society.

What impresses me in Barcroft's observation is his implicit sense for the relevance and usefulness of humanistic learning.

We are, after all, in a curious situation. We raise for discussion issues upon which, in point of fact, many of us act every day. We pretend not to know answers to questions which, in reality, we do answer in our everyday labor as students and teachers. Public discourse about the humanities is unsure and uncertain.[7] We have not found the appropriate language, nor the right questions. But the answers are there. We act with a certainty belied by our unsure rhetoric. We express ourselves—our thoughts and hopes, our philosophies and our writings—in a universal and practical way, and so we do, we practice, we apply the humanities. This is so even though, as is clear, when we say what we think we are doing, we resort to trite ideas and clichéd language. This is profoundly characteristic of the culture of our country: pragmatism and practicality in abundance, but a poverty of theory, a reticence of interpretation.

If that is so, then we have to work back from what we do to what we think we do. The movement has to be from the applied and practiced humanities, fully exposed and explained, to the theory of

---

[7]For example, it is difficult to point to first-class reporting of humanistic work as it is conducted either in universities or elsewhere. We have no journalistic tradition of what subjects constitute news. We do not know how we may so phrase the issues of humanistic learning and expression that the general public may be informed and invited to join in the discourse. So humanistic topics are treated as if they were something else, or, more often, are not treated at all. So there are no "events" worth reporting, except when they may be rephrased into something other than of a humanistic character. The obvious example is the persistently repetitious treatment of the succession of Joseph Duffey as chairman of the National Endowment for the Humanities, so that, whatever the issue, however long after the end of Ronald Berman's and the beginning of Joseph Duffey's chairmanship, we still hear the code-words, "elitists" and "populists." A further example is the inattention to humanistic topics (let alone achievements) of *The Chronicle of Higher Education*. A third is that there is a *Scientific American* but no *Humanistic American*.

CLEARING AWAY DEBRIS

humanistic application, and thence still further backward to that range of abstract definition which, at the moment, seems closed to us. The point of analysis must be in the applied humanities: *the tentative identification of things which we believe constitute the practice of humanistic learning and humanistic expression.* We have to begin with small things, the things about which we are confident. If, to take the most obvious point, we concur that those subjects catalogued by Congress do constitute humanistic subjects—even if these are not all humanistic subjects, and even if there is more to humanistic learning than happens in classrooms—we have before us an interesting problem of analysis. What is it that we think we learn in the study of these subjects? Specifically, what in these subjects teaches us about "the humanities" which is supposed to be shared by, and expressed through, them all? If it is philosophy, or linguistics, or the history and comparison of religions, or literature, the problem remains one. What is it that is that humanistic *thing?* Shall we call it a humanistic *residue? function? point in common?* or *trait?*

In point of fact, the problem, when phrased this way, is by no means so unfamiliar to any of us. True, we confront a problem of definition and interpretation, to define the humanities, to interpret their tasks and so to discover criteria for better, and for worse, in humanistic learning and expression. But is not this very task at the center of our humanistic work—clear description, penetrating analysis and interpretation? Whether the work is philosophy or history, there is the task of interpreting what has been done and explaining how it works and what it means. Now, to be sure, these subjects on the Congressional list are not the only ones in which there is a labor of description and interpretation to be done. As the systematic work of theoretical thought gets underway, something more will have to be said about what makes the humanities both alike among themselves and different from other intellectual disciplines and modes of expression. The worst thing we can do is to ask the right questions at the wrong time, to reach the conclusion before we have begun. Indeed, it is that error which seems to me to account for the present impasse on what is, in fact, a rather straightforward problem of thought.

"The unexamined life is not worth living." The same is so for those of us who practice "the humanities" and accept a paycheck for doing so. Since we make our living in this way, rather than in some other, we have to examine what we do and why we do it, if not day by day, then, at least, in moments of conscience and introspection. We presently are engaged in a considerable conversation on these subjects.

We have little experience in how to carry on just this kind of talk.[8] The whole area of public discourse in the humanities is uncharted, as Barcroft says.

But if we have not reached the beginning of the end, we have, at least, passed the end of the beginning: the subject is before us. The work is under way. As a rabbi in the Talmud says, "Yours is not to complete the work, but you are not free to ignore it." In my view the things we do define what we are doing. Those modes of critical thought and analysis which serve so well will have yet to serve again. If, after all, we can define and interpret a poem or a novel, a philosophical system or a historical event, the structure of a religion or the structure of a language, then surely we can answer just one more question. We should be able to say what it is that we think, do, for what purpose and to what end, when we define and interpret a poem, a system, or a structure.

---

[8] Perhaps all of us are too fearful of thinking old thoughts, because they are clichéd and trite. True, we are not going to sink to "the humanities are the study of man," but we need not be ashamed to say what has been said before, either.

CHAPTER 2
Defining the Humanities: From Many, One?

Practitioners of the humanities rightly take for granted that they know what the humanities are. But can we say what the humanities *is*? That is to say, there is common agreement on diverse subjects which fall within the category of the humanities: history, philosophy, religious studies, languages and literatures, and the like. But do these subjects and disciplines constitute a single thing, the humanities? If pressed, practitioners of these subjects will claim that what they have in common is the study of "man." That is to say, the proper study of the humanities is humanity. The commonality of the humanities is a shared subject. That is not much of a definition, invoking, as it does, the thing defined in the very definition, but it is deemed more or less adequate to the task.

Despite the banality of saying that what the humanities do is to study humanity, it indeed was adequate so long as the humanities remained essentially an academic exercise, a matter for university study only. University professors and students are not often pressed to define what they do in the humanities. There is a consensus, so there is no urgency in the matter. So long as diverse sorts of departments form a group without spending time debating, there is no harm at all in drawing together into the humanities a given set of departments, which (1) clearly do not practice social science, thus excluding economics, sociology, and political science, for instance, and (2) also do not fall into the range of mathematics, engineering, and natural sciences. True, we may undertake to debate the definition of a humanist. We may ask ourselves to accept the historical definitions of the humanities and the humanist in the framework of Western philosophy and culture. That is to say, the humanist, in the academic sense, is a person who fits into a tradition of humanistic research, going back to the Renaissance, with stress on the classics and philosophy. Now, as I said, all of this rather lazy and amiable discourse on what is a humanist, what is the humanities, and related subjects, is adequate to us in the backwaters of university life. Or, to state matters simply, we all know what we mean, even if (like college freshmen) we cannot say what we mean in an ample and clear way.

The fact that there is agreement not to press the matter too far began to present a serious impediment to public discourse when public discourse on the humanities, the state of the humanities, public programs in the humanities, the relevance of the humanities to the national welfare—when people began to care about the humanities. Public opinion started to ask that humanistic scholarship take on public responsibilities. For convenience's sake we can date this entry of humanities into public life with the creation of the National Endowment for the Humanities, fifteen years ago. But that date would prove misleading. For, after all, there have been state and public programs in humanistic learning from the beginnings of state and public education.

When we today contemplate the state of humanistic learning, we cannot limit our vision to universities and to professors and students. After all, we speak of the study of history, philosophy, religions, literatures and languages, and people study and practice these subjects not only in the classroom but also outside; not only in textbooks but also in magazines and newspapers and on television and in museums. The study of history is the work not only of professors and students, but of historical societies and museums, archives of all kinds, and ethnic and racial groups seeking a past and a future. In other words, the humanistic engagement of the society of this country and its public institutions is profoundly rooted, penetrating throughout the farthest reaches of our national life. We are a country which lives by humanistic reflection and expression.

In order to spell out the size of the humanistic constituency, let me describe the "universe" from which the National Endowment for the Humanities receives applications, as described in the most current (FY 1981) budget:

> —3,100 colleges and universities and 200,000 scholars and teachers of the humanities who serve them
> —16,000 public school districts and 17,000 independent schools, where Americans have their first (and half of them their only) exposure to the humanities
> —8,500 public libraries and 6,000 museums and historical organizations
> —250 public television and 200 public radio stations, and 3,750 independent media production groups, which provide means for bringing the humanities to great numbers of Americans throughout the country at low cost.

The same report continues:

> This "universe" touches a vast number of citizens, among them 50 million school children; 11 million students in college, university, and continuing

DEFINING THE HUMANITIES 15

education courses; the millions of Americans who watch and listen to the public media or who visit a museum or library each week; and the millions of citizens who participate in the discussion of issues of public policy and national concern.

When, therefore, we speak of the humanities, we address a critical and central sector of American public life.

The public interest in the humanities cannot be expressed better than it is in the relevant legislation, which creates the National Endowment for the Humanities (as well as the one for the Arts). Let me quote some of the language and an explanation of how this language shapes the work of the Endowment for the Humanities.

> In the National Foundation on the Arts and the Humanities Act of 1965, as amended, the Congress found, in its Declaration of Purpose. that "support of national progress and scholarship in the humanities . . . is . . . an appropriate matter of concern to the Federal Government"; that "a high civilization must . . . give full value and support to the . . . great branches of man's scholarly and cultural activity . . . "; that "democracy demands wisdom and vision in its citizens and . . . must therefore . . . support a form of education designed to make men masters of their technology . . . "; that "it is necessary and appropriate for the Federal Government to complement, assist, and add to programs for the advancement of the humanities . . . by local, State, and regional, and private agencies and their organizations"; that "the study of the humanities requires constant dedication and devotion and that . . . it is necessary and appropriate for the Federal Government to help create and sustain not only a climate encouraging freedom of thought, imagination, and inquiry, but also the material conditions facilitating the release of this creative talent"; and that "the world leadership which has come to the United States . . . must be solidly founded upon worldwide respect and admiration for the Nation's high qualities as a leader in the realm of the ideas of the spirit."
>
> These admirable purposes, translated into the terms of daily operations, impose on NEH two fundamental and complementary missions
>
> (1) to assist scholars and teachers in the humanities and the institutions which nourish their work in investigating the key questions in their scholarly disciplines, and to help them disseminate the products of their work through more effective teaching and publications; and
>
> (2) to foster, in the public at large, an awareness of the crucial issues in the humanities and of their importance for contemporary life in America.

As I have indicated, this country has created an Endowment for the Humanities, which itself is only the leading edge of public bodies—national, state, and local—in humanistic work, especially in applying the humanities to the concrete life of the country. The size of the constituency of humanistic activity is now clear. The dimensions of the public investment in humanistic work may only be imagined.

If, then, in light of all of this, we ask ourselves what the humanities are, and why they are relevant to national life, we surely have every right to expect to find answers. The ongoing labor of definition and self-criticism in humanistic learning and expression is simply a response to the ongoing public engagement with the humanities. When so much is done, should we not be able to explain why, not once for all time but day by day? For when we define, we explain. When we ask fundamental questions of definition, we bring to consciousness our deepest purposes. Such a work of definition is thus a process, not an event. It goes on whenever we attempt to say what we think we are doing and why we are doing it. Asking fundamental questions is the source of life for intellectuals, because it is the beginning of self-consciousness which is the trait of intellectuals. And, by definition, all humanists are intellectuals. The humanities is an exercise of mind.

The urgency of the matter of definition is clear. Billions of dollars are spent in programs and activities of a humanistic character. These funds come from federal, state and local governments and private agencies of every possible sort, including farm and labor unions, ethnic societies, local, regional and national groupings. Yet because of humanists' failure to undertake rigorous discourse on what we think we do when we do a humanistic deed (so to speak), we have not got language suitable to the reality of our activities. If, to give a concrete example, someone serves as director of the humanities for the Rockefeller Foundation or for a state-sponsored commission on the humanities, just what is that person's task? How shall we know what success consists of? And, finally, what good do these "humanities" do, that humanities should enjoy so much attention in government and in education?

If we now go back to where we started, we find our original definition difficult. We know that history, literature, philosophy and religion constitute subjects in the humanities. What we do not know is what unites them all, what is humanistic about each of them. We can concede that there are fifteen or twenty academic subjects which add up to "the humanities." We are much less sure that the humanities is something other, more than these fifteen or twenty academic subjects, one by one or added up and divided by fifteen or twenty. Consequently, our tendency is to resort to definition by example, saying that if one does this, that, or the other thing, it is "a humanity." Or, as I said at the beginning, we invoke the dreadful definition by banality.

The humanities are the study of humanity. But what it is *about* humanity which the humanities study, why the things the humanities do—severally or jointly—are worth doing, why the educational institutions and political agencies of this country should invest as vastly as they do in what the humanities study and the things they do—these are not questions which presently are raised urgently and in a rigorous way. So lacking definition, the humanities add up to yet one more pressure group, a constituency like any other, which demands its share of public support, alongside the social scientists and the natural scientists and diverse other intellectuals (people who make their living through what they know). Each of these sectors of the national cadres of culture lays claim to its place in the curriculum of schools and colleges, in the budget of states and federal government alike, and the basis for the claim of all of them is a few phrases, on the one side, and many votes, on the other. Where is there concern for moral authority or even public utility?

To move from a list of subjects which are humanistic to a definition of what the humanities is, we have to discover the things which draw the several subjects together. Let us work with a brief and simple list, which later on is to be expanded. History, literature, philosophy, and religion constitute humanistic subjects and disciplines. When we know what they have in common among themselves, and what separates them from other disciplines and subjects, we shall have moved a few steps toward the definition we seek. So a fair question is, What do I do, when I study history, literature, philosophy, and religions, which I do not do when I study biology, sociology, or astronomy?

One thing I do is rely essentially upon my insight, taste, and judgment. I form opinions which are not to be tested with mathematical abstraction or physical precision. Compared to the natural and social sciences, the humanities are a set of inexact bodies of learning. That is their pathos, why they are contentious. But it is also their power, why everyone wants to be a humanist.

A second thing I do when I study the four topics under principal discussion, which I do not do when I study the subjects of the natural and social sciences, mathematics, and engineering, is deal with something for which I can find an analogy in my own experience. When I read a work of literature or examine an artifact of a religion, I can find a metaphor for myself in what someone else has made. When I study the data of biology, I study what may be no less relevantly human. But what I study bears no analogy to what I can know, feel, think, touch, out of my own being. I study something wholly other. So the humanities deal with themes and topics to which we have access because we are human—I mean, direct access to knowledge and experience. In consequence, we construct bridges and analogies, paths of meaning from the thing we study to ourselves, in a way in which we cannot construct an analogy between the study of chemistry and the study of ourselves.

The oft-quoted statement that our bodies consist of a certain set of chemical substances makes the point full well. As long as a poet or philosopher has not got hold of that equation of what we are and our chemical composition, it is not an accessible or important statement. We are more than soap and lampshades, though we can be made into soap and lampshades. It is in the humanities that, through the minds of others and their feeling and imagination, we go in search of the difference.

Now this mode of thought, which isolates what I do as a practitioner of the humanities from what my colleagues do as practitioners of the social and natural sciences, mathematics and engineering, thus yields two simple observations I have made thus far.

First, the humanities are inexact sciences, which deal with matters of taste, judgment, feeling, and other things which are not to be weighed or measured, and which rarely are right or wrong in demonstrable and measurable ways.

Second, the humanities are those disciplines of mind which are constructed out of analogies between ourselves and what others have made or felt or thought, so that we personally and directly can enter into the subject—I mean the experience of mind—of history, literature, philosophy, or religions. This we do in ways which we personally cannot do when we enter the subjects of chemistry, biology or physics. Those subjects are "out there," so to speak, while the humanities are "in here," in our hearts and minds.

We can share the experience of a poem in a way in which we cannot experience a molecule or an equation. So the humanities are those disciplines or subjects which capture what it is to be what we are; I mean, the humanities speak about us in ways in which chemistry, physics, and biology speak about something other than us. To distinguish the humanities from the social sciences, in this context, need hardly detain us.

This matter of definition is not so simple as I have suggested, not only because of the self-evident limitations in the two components of a definition I just now offered. It also is not so simple because of the nature of what we do when we undertake the task of defining. As I said a moment ago, definition is an ongoing, never-ending task, because it is simply a way of asking the most fundamental questions of meaning and worth. When I define the humanities, it must be for a particular purpose. The definition is then measured by its adequacy to the purpose. At the same time, when I define the humanities, it is an effort to say not only what the humanities *is*, but also what the

DEFINING THE HUMANITIES 19

humanities is worth. A definition containing no element of evaluation and apology is not worth much. And, finally, when I define the humanities, I make a statement of *meaning* of the humanities, as much as one of *evaluation* of the humanities. The work is ongoing, as contexts change, and as the purpose of the exercise shifts.

When we consider the state of the humanities today, we must recognize that society has moved way beyond the sense of self-worth of academic humanists. There is a general and widespread appreciation for humanistic study and expression, an expectation that important questions of society and culture are addressed and even resolved through the humanities. That is why, as I said at the outset, there is that vast and great institution, the National Endowment for the Humanities, which itself is merely the tip of the iceberg of the federal engagement in humanistic education and expression. That is why every state has a commission on the humanities, funded in part by state, and in part by federal funds. That is why many cities, particularly in the south and west, as well as some county governments, have begun to take a second look at the promise and power of the humanities to make life still more worthwhile, for instance through support of museums and public TV. I daresay there is more faith in the humanities in the public mind, in the mind of legislators and political figures, than there is in the hearts of the academic and other professional humanists themselves That is why this labor of definition seems to me critical. It is not because people do not know what we do, or because they do not know the worth of what we do. It is because we do not adequately say what we think we do and why we claim it is important.

Any exercise in definition, therefore, will demand that we confront these two related questions: (1) the relevance of the humanities to the public interest, (2) the claim of the humanities upon the public interest. That is, we have to advance a claim to moral authority. For if we cannot explain why humanistic study and expression do not belong outside of the curriculum of the university, we also cannot account for the importance of the humanists within the academic curriculum. Academic life in this country sets upon a single continuum of a common culture. University students come from the encompassing society and return to it; there is no enclave which protects us and imparts to our work special rights of self-evident validity.

Now the demand to explain why the humanities are relevant and why society at large should support what we do and benefits from what we do do is not entirely fair. It also is a demand we readily can satisfy. Our reticence in this work of self-definition and apology has hardly reflected the power and glory of that which we define and explain.

Speaking once more of only four of the humanistic fields, history, literature, religions, and philosophy, we respond to the issue of relevance merely by stating what we do. Then the relevance is self-evident.

What could be more at the heart of contemporary life than the power of language to capture and set forth the truth and meaning of our life? The study of literature gives us direct access to the power of some great minds to use language to lay out the inner meaning of life.

What could be more at the center of contemporary discourse, what could be more practical, than the study of the history and the historical experience of humanity? From whom do we learn more important contemporary lessons than from historians, who lay out before us the potentialities of humanity, the record of what we have been, and what we might once more become?

The immediacy of philosophy, that bastion of clear and rigorous thinking about important questions, is easy to explain. A person who has not experienced the mode of thought and method of inquiry of a first-class philosophical mind is a person who does not know how to use the human mind.

Finally, what we study when we study religions are ways in which humanity has expressed its hopes and aspirations to be more than what it is, the modes by which people have constructed society and shaped a common life in response to the highest yearnings of the human spirit for transcendence. Religions present the social incarnation of the soul of societies. Should we not find the study of religions immediately relevant?

Society turns to the humanities, lavishes support upon them in schools and universities as well as in countless other ways, not because of the claim of humanists to superior culture. What society asks of us is to deal with the questions which form the focus of our labor anyhow, because those questions by nature define and express the critical issues of the day. I do not mean principally issues of abstraction, issues of meaning detached from practical concerns. I mean those intensely practical concerns of war and peace, the potentialities of society, the possibilities and requirements of clear thought, the character of self-consciousness and self-awareness—these dimensions of everyday life which tell us the measure of who we are, what we are, and how we may become something more than who and what we are.

So far as humanists speak of a crisis of the humanities and ask about how professional humanists—I mean, historians, philosophers, scholars of literature and religions—are to earn a living, they give evidence of the failure of a vision of the power and the promise of the humanities. A well-educated humanist—historian, philosopher, literary

DEFINING THE HUMANITIES 21

scholar, scholar of religious studies—has gifts of mind and sensibility which make such a person extraordinarily useful in all of the far reaches of employment. What is now gone is only the routine possibility of doing that for which one has been trained. Then we have to rethink the things for which we have been trained. The power of the philosopher, to use one example, is in the breadth and relevance of the outreach of philosophy—and these are without limit The humanities will overcome their transient crisis of employment when they transcend that passing mood of self-doubt brought on by a change from one mode of the social organization of learning to another such mode. The problems are institutional, not endemic to what is learned. There is no crisis of the humanities. There is a set of problems to be worked out by humanists. Given the substance and the promise of the humanities, the issues at hand, the solemnity of what is at stake, we who practice the humanities need not fear for our adequacy to the issues of relevance and to the social task at hand.

The truly formidable challenge is to retain that vision of the whole, that is, a conception of the humanities beyond this disciplinary field and that subject. It is altogether too easy for us to see each discipline of the humanities as a complete field in itself. We transform humanistic learning into an anti-humanistic technology. We use language not for communication of truth but for laying claim to status. When the study of literature loses sight of the issues captured and expressed by great writers, when the study of philosophy finds satisfaction in repeating formulas, when the study of history becomes the self-absorbed study of squabbles among historians, and when the study of religions loses all contact with what people do when they are religious, then technology takes over. We turn learning into the mere sociology of learning. The humanity of the humanities loses the center of the stage. Then we make use of scholarship not as a mode of attaining accurate and disciplined learning, but as a means to "do scholarship." We treat learning as a method of exalting the learned person, rather than as a means to exalt the subject of learning, which is humanity. Consequently, what we do loses all joy, all power of celebration. Then the practice of the humanities becomes not a profession of faith in the capacity of humanity to overcome its own limitations, but a mere profession, that is, something which one practices principally to make a living.

If there is a crisis in the humanities, it is not a crisis of the humanities, but only one of the excess of professionalization of humanists. That is why the call from the public sector, the call to explain and define ourselves, to spell out our use and value to the public interest, to explain why what we do is important and deserves a hearing—that is why that call touches the very core of our being. The crisis of definition of which we speak is a splendid opportunity to regain that clear and present purpose, that power of immediacy and relevance to the common task and the public interest, of which humanistic learning at its foundation, in its very topicality, consists. I began with one tautology, that the humanities study humanity. I end with another: the relevance of the humanities is to the humanity which is studied. The importance of the humanities finds its measure in the importance of ourselves, of our significant humanness. The public interest demands that this labor go forward, I mean, the labor of learning who we are and what we may become.

CHAPTER 3
Stranger at Home:
Toward a Theory of the Humanistic Study of Religion

I

If we do not ask ourselves tough questions about the intellectual and social worth of what we teach, we declare ourselves both intellectually bankrupt and socially irresponsible. This we cannot do while asking society for its children to teach and for its resources to support our teaching. I find myself impatient, therefore, when told that any subject, whether religion or biology, is "intrinsically" interesting. I am prepared to concede that all subjects are intrinsically interesting. But I do not know what value there is in such a concession. For we have to make choices, and so does society. It will not do to commend everything and decline nothing. We must exercise taste and judgment. We must also explain the result. That is self-evidently not an argument in favor of a pragmatic or narrowly utilitarian approach to learning. But neither is it going to give comfort to scholars who disdain to teach, teachers who prefer to preach, or faculties which become lazy, unresponsive, and indifferent to their tasks both in education and in scholarship.

No one can hope that there are lasting answers to the question, Why should I know the things which you are telling me? But the generation of teachers and scholars which does not try to answer fails both those who came before and those who are to come.

II

The starting point of any answer should be the educational results we hope to achieve. That result will be in two parts: first, with reference to students in general, whatever their majors, and second, with reference to majors in our field.

The former group is far more important than the latter, for the reason I implied at the outset. Our interest is to provide something of cultural and intellectual value to a wide variety of students, to serve the entire community of our university. Given the vocational choices which govern curricular decisions made by the generality of students everywhere, we are not going to see massive numbers of students in our more specialized courses. They will study other things. Most of them will not earn a living from what they learn from us, nor will what we have to teach in concrete ways make them more useful in their chosen business, profession, or calling. My own impression, moreover, is that students who come to us from mathematics and the natural sciences tend to be more engaging, because, by the nature of things, in the world about which we speak, they also are both uninformed and rather unformed. Since my own university has impressive numbers of students in pre-medical studies as well as in engineering, mathematics, and the natural sciences, and very large numbers of other students who plan to become lawyers or to go to business school, I must ask myself questions of purpose in a context quite different from that in which colleagues in biology or applied mathematics explain why someone should want to know what they teach.

Our situation in the study of religions is characteristic of the humanities in general. It is our task to shape Religious Studies within the humanities in such a way that they win the attention of students engaged by other things, and cause them to be willing to learn what we have to teach. It is one thing to win attention. It is another to teach something worthy of attention. Ours is the work of doing both. Yet it remains to observe that the generality of our students see us for one or two or three courses, while they pursue their major fields for eight or ten or twelve courses. The result is that Religious Studies, for the main part of their student constituency, take the form of courses which survey a fair amount of material for a sizable number of students, courses which meet a requirement, and from which students themselves demand somewhat more than they do of their majors: to tell them whatever they should know, while, so to speak, we stand on one foot (if not on our heads).

This demand is an opportunity and a challenge. It requires us to ask, Among the many important and pressing things I wish to share out of what I know, what are the most urgent? Every time we plan a course, we select the few things we can manage in the twelve or fourteen weeks we have. This act of selection, which begins when we claim to do our subject for more than its "intrinsic" interest, continues in the many acts of selection by which we frame our courses, the topics of our lectures, the readings we put into students' hands.

Before proceeding to outline these urgent matters, I call to mind that other, rather select group of students, our majors in Religious Studies. Since these students only occasionally plan to enter the priesthood, ministry, rabbinate, or other religious vocations and careers, in their vocational character they are not so different from the students whom we serve in a few survey or general courses. Moreover, most of them take so wide a variety of courses within Religious Studies that nearly every course they elect also turns out to be elementary. If an advanced course is one which demands a prerequisite of some other, prior course, we almost always teach beginners. For an examination of catalogues yields very few second or third courses in our field. Many of these allegedly advanced courses turn out to be just as elementary as the others. There may be an "introductory" course, required of all students. But, commonly, in no way does such a course pretend to introduce all the other courses students may take. It hardly lays down foundations on which the other courses within the departmental curriculum are going to build. Our field is too specialized, too diverse in its methods. It follows that the bulk of our teaching serves students who ask absolutely fundamental questions, one of which must always be, Why are you telling me these things? Why should I know them? How shall I be changed because I know them?

III

We live in an age of intense faith and of utter indifference about religions. Our work is important both to the faithful and to those for whom religious belief and behavior bear no this-worldly interest whatsoever. Our work is not to reshape the faith of the faithful, nor to kindle interest in the uninterested. It is different. When we say we stand at a distance from the subject, claim to be objective about the "truth-claims" of the religions we study, or solemnly affirm that we do not serve, or violate, the interests of organized religion or of atheism, our protestations are true but they miss the point. What we do in general is simply not suitably described or explained within the frame of reference expressed in terms of faith or unfaith, commitment or doubt, even concern or unconcern about the subject. What we do is to try to interpret the phenomenon of religions as a force in human life.

To answer the question, Why Religious Studies? we have to ask another: What do people *not* know, if they do not know about and understand religions? What can they *not* explain and of what can they not make sense? Phrased in this way, the question answers itself. For religion is so powerful a force in the contemporary world that without knowledge of religion we scarcely can understand the daily newspapers. A fair example of what happens when people do not know how to make sense of the power of religions in contemporary life is our country's difficulty in understanding the Islamic revolution in Iran, not to mention the Judaic revolution in the State of Israel, the Protestant army of Northern Ireland, the Roman Catholic revolution in Poland and in Latin America, the Christian army of Lebanon, the tragedy at Jonestown, and many continuing evidences of the vitality of religious belief—sometimes healthy, sometimes perverse.

There is of course a bias against religion as a force in culture and psychology. This is surely one possible way of thinking about the character and meaning of society and of life. It holds religion to be dying, a holdover from another age. It therefore claims that religion does not require study. Those of us who find religion an exceptionally interesting phenomenon of society and culture, imagination and the heart, can do little to overcome this bias. But it *is* a bias, for it rests upon the will to wish religion away, not upon the perception that religion has gone away. In fact, much of the world as we know it is shaped by the formation of society and culture around religious beliefs, by the way in which people refer to religions to make their choices about how they will live. These beliefs and choices invoke particular modes of supernaturalism, distinctive expressions of revelation. A country governed by a president who speaks of a personal experience of conversion had better understand the meaning of religious conversion. A nation in which institutions of religion exercise vast influence over citizens' political and cultural decisions is not wise to deny that religion is a formative force in contemporary life. Whether or not people want religions to exercise that power, they do. In fact, religions not only speak about supernatural powers, they, too, constitute powerful forces in this world.

So it is a matter of fact that if people do not understand the character of religions, they cannot make sense of much which happens in the world today. Nor need we dwell upon a still more obvious fact. To understand where humankind has been, to make sense of the heritage of world civilization, the transcendent side of the human imagination and of society and culture constitutes a definitive dimension. There is no understanding of humanity without the confrontation with the religious heritage and hope, whatever may be our judgment of the value of the heritage and the hope. So far as universities propose to teach how to interpret the world in which we live, organizing courses and Departments of Religious Studies is a perfectly natural way of teaching what must be taught.

IV

To this point in the argument I have tried to explain two of the three elements mentioned earlier, spelling out whom we teach and explaining what we teach, that is, transmit facts, ideas, and insight about important things. We have now to try to speak of the particular things we do in Departments of Religious Studies. It is axiomatic that we do not produce more faithful, or less faithful, Christians, Jews, Moslems, Buddhists, and the like. But it is equally clear that we do claim to attempt to explain these powerful forces in human culture which we call religions.

The task of explanation is accomplished through three distinct approaches to learning—history, philosophy, and social science. Each approach to the study of religions is indispensable. None exhausts the possible approaches to the work. In the area of history, we ask about the role and development of diverse religions within diverse cultures, within the life of various peoples, regions, and territories. Work in this area tends to rely upon literary evidence, for example, holy books, although archaeologists have begun to teach us to take seriously non-literary evidence. In the area of philosophy we analyze the language and claims about truth put forward in various religions; we ask about the ethics laid forth, and speak of the perennial issues of religious truth phrased in terms applicable to any culture. In social scientific approaches we inquire into the social setting and impact of a religion, on the one side, and into religions' psychological meaning, the place of religion in the life of the imagination and emotion, on the other. The enduring classics of theory of religions, for instance, the works of Freud, Weber, and Durkheim, have come from the fields of psychology and sociology of religions. Nor is the study of religions complete without the learning of anthropologists, who, like historians of religion, reach out to alien people, to people who, though living in the present, are foreign to our age, speaking in a strange language, about things we know not what. Anthropologists teach us to understand in common human terms the system, structure, and order of this alien world in our midst.

In this rapid account of the main disciplines of Religious Studies, we have also to catalogue the sorts of data to be analyzed by scholars of the field. Since human beings express transcendent impulses in every medium of access, scholars of religion have to teach themselves to recognize and hear these expressions wherever they occur. That is why the study of literature of the present and past, of art of today and yesterday, of music, drama, dance, poetry, cinema, as much as of sociology and anthropology, makes formidable contributions to the description and interpretation of religions. Nor may we omit notice of the important lessons to be learned from specialists in fields in which data of religions play only a peripheral part. It is not possible to understand the religions of the West without studying Western civilization, just as one cannot understand the civilization of the West without intimate knowledge of religious institutions and expectations. So we come to our colleagues in history for assistance in our work. Political science, with its insight into how religious convictions and origins play a role in social and political behavior, provides ample data for the examination of religion as a vital and powerful force in contemporary life. Since art, music, and literature give access to what is happening in the soul of a society, there is no way to ignore the sizable work to be done in these departments of learning.

By now the picture is obvious. When we ask what we do in the study of religions, we discover ourselves in the very center of a field of learning which, at its foundations, is interdisciplinary and cross-cultural. It relies so heavily upon so wide a range of disciplines as to be declared the quintessential form of humanistic learning. Religious Studies cast a net over land and sea and everywhere find treasure. Whether or not there is a discipline distinctive to the study of religion I do not know. I am certain that there is no discipline of the academic curriculum in humanistic and social studies which Religious Studies can afford to neglect. This is surely so if we wish to understand this protean force, this ubiquitous thing, religion. For to study religion is to study humanity in its full humanness: integrated and whole, but frail, vulnerable, full of fantasies and fears, and in perpetual quest. It is no wonder that one religion finds its evocative symbol in a criminal in his death throes, and another finds its vindication in the very suffering of its communicants. In these ways and in others Christianity and Judaism, among the religions of humanity, express that vulnerability and frailty which, through religions, humankind has sought to express and overcome.

V

Thus far I have explained what I believe to be the remarkable power of Religious Studies: first, their capacity to make their own nearly the entire spectrum of humanistic, and most of the social scientific, disciplines of learning, and, second, their reason for studying virtually every kind of expression of our humanness. But the power of the field is also its problem and its pathos. If we attempt to do so much, shall we not do most of it superficially, and the rest incompetently? That question by no means is to be dismissed. When, years ago, our department searched for a scholar in the social scientific approach to the study of religions, we found it difficult to locate an appropriate social scientist willing to join us. The more intelligent ones preferred to be sociologists of religion in departments of sociology. The sociologists who wanted to join us did not find academic sociology engaging. And the work of both sorts—with its stress on counting and measuring things—seemed to us not very interesting anyhow. But whatever the difficulties Religious Studies depend, perhaps more than the study of most other humanistic subjects, upon help from colleagues. Indeed, we constantly refer to colleagues in other disciplines, both to teach us how they do their work, and to guide us in doing our own. The interdependence of Religious Studies with other disciplines of the humanities and social sciences is a powerful argument for the formation of a distinct department, such as this one. But it is a still stronger argument that, once the department has discovered its identity and purpose, its task is to reach out to colleagues with an interest in the thing we study and with much to teach us about it and about how to study it.

It is one thing to say that we are interested in everything. But it is quite another to specify the things that, in general, scholars in Religious Studies do well, and to confess the things which, in general, they tend to do poorly. So any account of the field as it takes up its duties in a new department of Religious Studies must address this very question. I see four principal sins of Religious Studies in the past twenty years.

The problems we tend to treat expertly are familiar ones. They derive from Western civilization. The kinds of sources we handle with skill normally are literary. The issues in the study of religions we confront with confidence arise from the Christian and Western philosophical perspectives upon religious experience and thought. In other words we do well what we know, less well what we do not. So while we may rightly claim to be interested in everything, we are disingenuous if we offer that claim at face value. This is the first of four sins of Religious Studies. The field's diffuse character conceals its cultural sameness, its origins in Protestant divinity schools. To observe that the curriculum of a fair number of departments, particularly in smaller, church-related colleges, replicates too accurately the principal interests of divinity faculties, is to bring no news. To point out that an alternative in both scholarship and teaching has yet to be worked out and made to stick is another matter.

Our vision of the subject remains pretty much what it was. We have the breadth of concern which is the virtue of the Protestant conscience. But we also exhibit the incapacity to attain critical self-consciousness, the conviction of majorities that how we see things is pretty much how they are, which is the vice. The caring for all things is formed into a utensil of one shape only, by limited sympathy. No one has to choose a position of entire relativity of values to notice that, in the study of religions, we tend to bring a rather limited program of interests and concerns. That is why some, who work on religions essentially unlike Protestant Christianity, turn to anthropology for categories of inquiry. We find the narrowly theological, intellectual definition of issues of Religious Studies to be of limited utility. That is why others turn to approaches borrowed from other data, for instance, structuralism as a mode of interpreting ritual. The inherited, philosophical categories of the field do not present a viable hermeneutic for religions as they are practiced outside of this country's Protestant churches and culture.

A further trait of the field derives, if by somewhat remote connection, from yet another strength of Protestant culture: the power to respond to the events of the moment. It is its capacity to remain relevant to a changing world, to address each hour afresh, which has made Protestant culture so functional to the industrial West. A natural attitude of mind in our field is to respond quickly and relevantly to what happens in ways which some of us, out of more "traditional" cultures, find admirable. At the same time Religious Studies as a field tend to go from hula-hoop to frisbee, taking as evanescent slogans ideas which the framer means to be handled very seriously indeed. After twenty years in the field of Religious Studies I have learned to approach with measured enthusiasm the intellectually-salvific theories of the moment. When I find at the American Academy of Religion pretty much a single slogan sweeping from one section to the next— whether it is "the social construction of reality," or "phenomenology," or "structuralism," or even something so specific as black, women's or Jewish perspectives on Religious Studies—I go back to my room and watch television. For there at least the fads are an honest way to make a living.

What is wrong with the perpetual faddism and sloganeering of the field is not that slogans contain no truth or convey no insight. It is that in our faddism we forget the roots of the academic study of religions. What is new in the marketplace of ideas turns out to be a repackaging of what is old. The second sin of the field thus is academic consumerism. How many steps do we take, after all, from Durkheim to Douglas? And how far a journey do we travel from Weber to Bellah and Geertz? The classicism of the Judaic tradition and of the Roman Catholic form of Christianity—to name accessible modes of belief—has yet to make its contribution to the shaping of attitudes of mind in our nascent discipline. Only in preserving the tension between the claims of the exciting new and the doubts of the experienced old shall we succeed in retaining some sort of balance and prudence in our intellectual venture.

The methodological diffuseness of the field, which is its strength, exacts a price in an absence of critical self-consciousness, on the one side, and an excess of contemporaneity, on the other. It tends to yield yet another good thing which also is bad: a general education. In those universities which lack programs in Western civilization, the study of two subjects tends to take their place: history, in the form of the general survey course, and religious studies, in the form of the introductory course, e.g., to Catholicism, Protestantism, and Judaism, or to the religions of the West, or, still grander, to the religions of the whole world. Surely it is an act of responsibility and of courage for our faculties to undertake these kinds of courses. Student response as well as collegial approval (for others do not wish to tread where we happily proceed) gratifies and rewards us. If, because of its integrated and wide-ranging topicality, the study of religions serves as a kind of general education, it also replicates the dubious intellectual traits of general education. Our general, introductory courses—often the only ones our students elect—leave the impression of breadth, when they make a superficial mark; appear to speak of important things, when they raise issues which are merely relevant; and evoke the language of eternity, but speak, in the end, of how we feel today. These are bitter judgments. They judge as much what I do as anyone else.

The third sin is that in our teaching we are mere generalists, when we should be specialists speaking in accessible, general terms—a very different thing. We talk about too many things. This is bad not merely because about most we come armed only with our impressions. It also is bad because we lose the power to criticize ourselves, even to distinguish bad from good in our own thought and understanding. I am unhappy, for example, at how little effort goes into the careful and sympathetic reading of the texts of alien religions. It is as if we wish to get the gist of an ancient tablet without making sense of the glyphs of the alien alphabet. It cannot be done. Meaning must be expressed in words. Words come in one language or another, governed by a specific syntax and intimate grammar of thought and idiomatic expression. Those of us who teach what is not commonly familiar, because we tend to be embarrassed at the alienness of our texts, leap over the specificities into a common language of thought. We chatter in a kind of intellectual Esperanto which no one really uses at all.

We have not figured out how to teach some one or two texts, in a given course, which will say things beyond themselves, yet distinctive and particular to themselves. It is exceedingly difficult to find the modalities between technical gibberish (which would then place us in graduate seminars of philology) and insufferable banality (which leaves us right where we are). To put matters more simply: I do not yet know the way which leads from telling my students about King Upupalupu to informing them that "Deep down, people really are good, anyhow." In the interstices between knowing how to read and interpret a text or some other datum of religion (a play, a dance, a rite, a prayer), and knowing how to talk to the concerns of the hour and of the particular age through which the students now pass, lies that kind of teaching which, right now, is difficult to define: teaching students something worth knowing.

The fourth and last sin is most serious. No indictment of Religious Studies as an academic field can fail to charge that we have played our full part in the destruction of the study of foreign languages in America. If I have to point to the single indefensible achievement of our field (it is no defense that we did not do it all by ourselves), it is the propagation of the notion that we can understand what is alien without learning the language of the alien. Our sin is not merely the absence of requirements that our majors learn some language relevant to their studies of religions. It is a failure at the very center of our mission which allows our students to assume that they understand things to which, in fact, they do not even gain access.

Our work is to make what is strange into something human, to teach how to make sense, in *its* alien terms, of what some among us too soon make their own. The study of religions, when not wholly subjective, and therefore not academic to begin with, is the study of the religious life of others. It is not the religious life of the teacher of a given classroom or of every student in that classroom. The other, to be understood, cannot be reduced to ourselves. We have to allow the other to be different—and then to confront and attempt to overcome the difference without dissolving it. It is no news to declare that the work of the humanities is to examine the diversity of human experience and to ask what is human about humankind. But how are we to confront diversity and take differences seriously, when we do not even know that other people talk of things we know not what, in languages which to us are gibberish. The first step in any humanistic venture of learning must be to allow the other to be alien, yet to seek for what is like ourselves in the alien. The final step is to understand more than that the stranger is in ourselves. It is to realize, also, that we are in the stranger.

Now it is one thing to tell people things. It is another for people to experience them. I can think of no more direct, experiential encounter with the specific issues of the humanities than in learning a foreign language. For the beginning of that process of learning to seek in the language we want to learn analogies and metaphors for the language we already know. But the end of that learning is when the language we want to learn takes on its own reality in our ears, eyes, and mouths, so that we make the alien tongue into our own. When we deprive our students of the opportunity to enter into an alien language, we deprive ourselves of the occasion to teach what we really know, which is more than what our students already know.

In reading finals in my courses I am struck by how many could have been written without taking my courses at all. Students do not hear, because they do not understand that we are not telling them things they already know, even when we may say words they have already heard. I am astonished at how much which to me seems fresh and new enters the students' ears in accord with patterns of thought and definitions of issues established far away and long before they come to me. Many times I try to say, "If you think you already know this, you are not understanding what I am saying." But where can I evoke that consciousness of *not* understanding which must precede the process of seeking understanding among people who have never heard in their lives a foreign word or an alien thought? For students must first learn to be strangers to themselves, before they can see the given as chosen and new, and themselves as free to make choices.

To be sure, this country is not a monolingual society. Each region is rich in its own culture and speech. All parts of the country benefit from the presence of communities which speak some language other than American English. But we tend to ignore what we do not understand and to suppose that we all say pretty much the same thing in the same way. In fact we talk past one another, each about something the other could not make sense of, even if it were explained.

We in the humanities vindicate our work because it teaches people how to think. The very absence of a vocational tie between our subject and the students' future justifies what we do. Yet if we are training minds, then alongside those skills in clear thinking and accurate expression which we seek to cultivate belongs the direct experience of the alien which comes only in learning a text in its own language. It is not merely because when students never encounter the language other people use they do not do the hard work of cultural interpretation. It is more especially because of something more particular to our own field. When students do not realize, in their own direct experience of the alien, that nearly everything we have reaches us in a labor of translation and mediation, they do not grasp what is at the core of the study of religions. At the center of our intellectual enterprise is this same work—the translation and mediation of alien experience. This is what the study of a foreign language, properly carried out, makes available: the struggle to understand, to make sense in our language, of what is not our own.

VI

What makes the study of religions difficult is also what makes the work important. The principal difficulty is that the students all take for granted they know that about which we are talking. Nearly all of them come from one or another of the religious traditions of the West. Many of them have strong opinions on religions and on questions of theology. So they think they know already what we have to tell them. That is the challenge. But it also is what makes our work important. For, as I shall now argue, the crucial thing we can give, which our students badly need, is the encounter with the unfamiliar in what they take for granted. We can show them that what they think they know contains much yet to be learned. We can demonstrate that the absolute, wholly familiar given of life—that matter of religion—contains within itself a great many choices. Once we persuade them that, within religious expressions, people make important choices about the sort of society and culture they will sustain and the kind of people they will build, we provide them with an insight into their own most urgent task, namely, to learn how to make choices about things which seem settled and decided, to see as strange and new, requiring reflection and thought, what has all the time appeared familiar, routine, and closed. In the experience of discovering the familiar to be strange and to require analysis, our students undergo the experience of intellectual maturing which prepares them for a deeper, inner movement toward adulthood. My claim therefore is not a small one. I argue that the academic study of religions, because of its particular character, presents a splendid opportunity for our students to experience in intellectual terms what in fact is their most profound and pressing personal responsibility: the discovery of self, the engagement with their own individuality. What we do is relevant, in the deepest sense, to the students' task of attaining adulthood.

Let me explain. It is this matter of the encounter with what is not our own which, when our work succeeds, we may declare to be educational success and, when our work does not succeed, we recognize as failure. At the outset I argued that the reason the study of religions belongs in the center of the curriculum is that religions are a powerful and ubiquitous force in humankind. But what it is about religions which we need to master for the sake of useful knowledge remains to be stated. This is to be explained in two aspects. I have, first, to say why we think our students in particular ought to know about the things we teach. I must explain, second, why the society and community we serve ought to know them.

Since our students in the main are late adolescents, our work is defined by the psychological and emotional context of that age-group, as much as by its vocational or even cultural aspirations. Indeed, in any group of university students, however carefully selected, I am inclined to wonder whether many even *have* vocational and cultural goals. But all of them are engaged by how they feel, what they think about themselves, and what their peer group thinks about them.

Now the power of the study of religions is that, in our society, we speak of kinds of familiar experiences. It is difficult to grow up in America without knowing that there are churches and synagogues, religious myths and symbols of various kinds, to which various folk respond in diverse ways. There are experiences of religious conversion and rebirth, rites of birth and puberty, teachings about what one may do and must not do, and institutions for the expression and embodiment of all of these things. It follows that our students know that about which we are talking when we speak about religions. That is our richest asset. But it also is the most formidable obstacle to teaching our students something worth their knowing.

To explain, I must emphasize that what young people approaching maturity require is the capacity finally to surpass themselves, leaving childish things, while retaining the heritage of family, home, and love. They have to learn how to make their own what others have made for them, so to enter, finally, into the life of maturity and responsibility. They come to us as dependents upon their parents. They leave to take up their own careers. In the four years they spend with us, we have to guide them from dependence to independence. It is this supererogatory work of helping in the process of maturing which, in many instances, is our richest gift to our students.

If in intellect we can confront them with an authentic experience of attaining self-consciousness and of critically, thoughtfully evaluating what they think they already know in the encounter with what they do not know—the "alien experience" to which I referred earlier—then we allow for a controlled experiment of maturing. That is to say, through their intellectual labor we guide them in paths which, by analogy and metaphor, lead where life demands they go.

To state the matter simply: they already know about religions, more commonly, "their" religion. But they do not know what they know, or even that they know. For in the main knowledge about religions is acquired through inarticulate experience, on the one side, or through indoctrination, on the other. In both ways it is unreflective; the learner is dependent. The students think they know and understand things they do not know of their own knowledge. That is why they tend to assume they understand what we are saying. They assume they have already heard what in fact (in our minds) is fresh and unprecedented for them.

When we help students attain the clear capacity to distinguish new from old, the act of understanding from mere assent, the conscious deed of interpretation from the presumption of dumb familiarity, we lead them in mind through the very center of their existential task of growing up. I do not mean we make them less religious or more religious than they were, let alone better or worse Christians or Judaists. I mean we show them that there is more to be learned about what they think they already know, and that they can learn it. It is the experience of that kind of independence of intellect which will both prefigure and replicate the independence of personal existence each student has, in a brief time, to attain.

VII

Explaining why society and our community ought to know what we have to teach comes at the end. Our own country has entered upon a period in its history much like that of the late adolescent, approaching the decisions of maturity. For a long time, like children, we pretended there was no world but our own. Then, in World War II and afterward, we pretended that the whole world was our own. Now is the time to come to terms with a world which is not our own, but in which we have a share. To recognize both what is ours and what is not ours is to understand what is foreign but what we can make our own.

It is this encounter with the alien which requires our community and society to take up the intellectual and cultural tasks of interpretation of what we do not understand out of the resources of what we deeply comprehend. This social and political task of making ourselves at one and whole with an alien world is something we cannot do, if we have not experienced the work in some small place. In the study of religions which are not ours we learn how to enter into worlds which belong to others.

That is why the importance of learning a foreign language and of learning about a religion other than our own is the same: it is to prepare us for the confrontation with difference, to educate our sympathies to welcome diversity, to discover what we can be in what we are not. We must learn to glory in the encounter with difference, not only because we have not got any choice. The reason is also that we should not want it otherwise. In finding out things we did not know, we learn. In encountering and entering into worlds we did not make, we discover. In the learning and discovery, we uncover in ourselves things we did not know were there. We find out we can be more than what we are.

The critical task facing this country in the world and in our life as a nation is to learn to confront difference. Our society now recognizes that there is no single normative culture for all of us to accept. Twenty per cent of the population speaks Spanish. Nearly twelve per cent is black. Three per cent is Jewish. There is a growing minority of Moslems and Buddhists, both native and immigrant. I have the privilege of sitting on the National Council on the Humanities, governing body of the National Endowment for the Humanities, and so I always am studying proposals of many sorts, from many kind of groups and organizations, in every part of the country. I marvel at the diversity. I am amazed that before us come the ideas of men and women who know how to find the humanist in all of us.

The world in which we live no longer concedes that one way of life or one system is valid for all. The world for which our students now prepare demands, therefore, the capacity to take two steps, first, to discover oneself in the other, so that the alien seems less strange, and second, to discover the other in oneself, so that the self seems more strange. When our students study a religion other than the one in which they were brought up, they discover themselves in what is different. They undertake the exercise of empathetically interpreting the alien in terms which allow for their act of understanding. When they study the religion in which they were brought up and for the first time undertake the task of sympathetic, academic analysis and interpretation, they discover the alien in what they thought belonged to them. Questions which seem settled long ago turn out to be unsettling. The alien is within. Where we are most at home, there we are mostly strangers.

If our notion is that we study with profit only someone else's religion, we deprive ourselves of what we most require. To take one example, if contemporary Jews take for granted that they also know all about and define Judaism, they transform themselves from isolated and not necessarily representative or consequential facts about a given religion, Judaism, into the measure of all things Judaic. They reduce a complex tradition, going back for nearly three millennia, into only its most current, and not demonstrably its most representative form. The same is so for Christians. It is when our students realize that even what they think they know best, themselves and their own culture, contains mysteries yet to be uncovered that our work begins. It is when we understand that, in the work of learning, we remain perpetually outsiders in our own richly complex traditions, strangers when we feel most at home, that our work begins.

CHAPTER 4
NEH Occasions:
Who Chooses?

The decision-making process of the National Endowment for the Humanities answers the simple question, in three parts: (1) who decides (2) who gets what (3) for what purpose? When you realize that NEH disposes of nearly $150M annually, thirty times more than the budget of the largest corporate foundation, Exxon Education Foundation, you realize the magnitude of the decisions.

If, for instance, a field is deemed too small or unimportant, it will be denied all access to federal support for its scholars, publications, conferences, exhibits, in all, for the creation of its intellectual substance and the dissemination thereof. If, on the other hand, a field is deemed critical to "the national interest," money will flow to its specialists.

That obvious fact makes us wonder whether there is discussion about "national cultural policy," when and how someone decides that one field is more important than some other. A year ago investigators working in behalf of the House Appropriations Committee criticized the National Endowment for the Humanities for its failure to define a national policy for the humanities. The Endowment's leadership at that time responded that the one thing NEH does not want to do is declare who in the humanities will live and who will die: to be a "ministry of culture."

And yet, if there is no national policy for the humanities, still decisions are made every day, and funds go for one purpose and not for some other. Consequently, so far as people make decisions to spend on one matter or for one scholar's proposals instead of on some other's, they carry out an existing policy or they make a new one. There is no choice.

In the Endowment the prevalent attitude (which I share) is one of service, search for "underserved constituencies," and an eagerness to reach out with programs of significant humanistic substance. So far as there is a policy, therefore, it is an inchoate but nonetheless consistent interest in outreach, in public service in the best sense.

Indeed, the one unanticipated development after fifteen years of NEH history is the formation of a corps of public servants highly skilled in the promotion of the humanities and in the administration of programs of humanistic interest. The accumulation of know-how and the mastery of the art of effective use of public funds for humanistic purposes—these are the achievements of people who staff the Endowment. The increment of wisdom and understanding endures from one administration to the next. It originates in self-criticism and highly self-conscious reflection on what has worked and what has not.

To give one instance of this fact, I cite staff comment, in selected project evaluations, not only on what has been done in a given project, but what has been learned, in a general way, for other projects.

(1) An ongoing issue before the Endowment is how to decide which projects should receive what amounts to long-term, even permanent support, and which should not. In evaluating one such long-term project, the program officer went in search, as she said, "of a valuable lesson for the Agency. . . . The participation of the [host] University in this project is crucial. Were it not for their intervention, it is unlikely that such an apparently 'esoteric' project . . . could successfully raise significant funding from the private sector. . . . This grant has been remarkably free of adminstrative difficulties and requires comparatively little [NEH] staff time. . . . That would not be so if the field of . . . were less cohesive or set lower standards on the products of its members. . . . " What these comments indicate is that the program officer has raised questions of policy in the examination of a specific project, so that from the concrete experience yielded by one long-term activity, the Endowment may learn useful generalizations.

(2) In the same set of project evaluations a program officer reports how he recognized a national problem—the absence of a specialty of ethical studies in a particular area of applied science—and went about bringing into being the systematic study of ethics in that area.

(3) To take yet a third example of the accumulation of know-how, the Endowment now undertakes the cataloguing and preservation of newspapers held in libraries and archives in the fifty states and territories. How do you begin? The one way is *not* to announce a program and give grants. It is a careful, step-by-step procedure, by which we accumulate knowledge of how things work in one area—one state—and how to discern the dimensions and value of such an immense, yet self-evidently critical, program.

If up to now you think that it is the NEH staff which decides who gets support for what purpose, you will have reached a conclusion roundly and vigorously rejected by the Endowment. And here is the critical matter. The staff and administration argue that the decision on how public money is spent lies in the hands of "outside experts," that is, representatives of the fields under study and experts in them. These experts, assembled in panels, read the applications and evaluate them. Their comments are (merely) summarized and written up by the staff. These then are passed on upward to the National Council on the Humanities. The Council, meeting in committees supervising each of the Endowment's operating divisions, receives these reports and decides on recommendations to be brought to the Council's general session. Resolutions advising the chairman on the disposition of every application (both for funding and not for funding) come before the Council. The chairman cannot make a grant in excess of $17,500 (in the present legislation) without a Council recommendation. So the Council stands smack in the center of the decision-making process.

If then you want to know how the Endowment describes its decision-making process, you will look in vain for the (self-effacing) staff. They are merely competent "facilitators," people who receive applications, send them out for expert evaluation by reviewers, convene panels of representative and important scholars, and collect, organize, and hand on the judgments of these panels to the august members of the Council committee assigned to their respective divisions. So the staff represents itself as essentially ancillary.

Now that representation on the face of it conflicts with the first-rate staff work which makes an encounter with the NEH truly exceptional. For NEH is famous for the efficiency, professionalism, courtesy, and commitment of its staff—rightly so. From mere "facilitators" who expects true professionalism? Why should people who merely carry papers and opinions from one authority to some other, higher authority, present us with their insights into what works and what does not? How are we to make sense of the brilliant initiatives, in bringing into being a specialty in ethics, in calling into existence a massive project to preserve the journalistic heritage of the nation—how are we to make sense of such initiatives, if they really come from mere clerks and bureaucrats?

The fact is that the NEH staff is far too expert in the formation and implementation of the humanistic-cultural policy of this country to be deemed mere clerks. In fifteen years, as I said, a highly skilled cadre of experts in the administration of humanistic affairs has come into being. It has developed its own sense of what is valuable and what is not.

The staff moreover has discovered a community of interest with its constituency (or part of it). The staff will systematically select those experts it deems to have first-class opinions and ignore the views of those it regards as unimportant, idiosyncratic, or embarrassing. Now the one who decides who decides who gets what and for what purpose is the one who really governs. If I can formulate the agenda and decide what questions are asked, I do not much care about the answers. If I can choose who makes the choices, I already have defined the boundaries of what is permitted and what is not. If I wanted to build a ministry of culture, I should not want to address and sign Treasury checks, for I need not do so. Just let me choose the ones who make up the lists of reviewers of applications and who collect and call together panels to advise on the disposition of applications. All the rest is mere shouting.

Now smack in the heart of the matter, the make-up of panels, sits what we should expect in our day and age: a computer. In the computer are about twenty thousand names and resumes, and from the computer come the proposed experts for a given application's review and for making up a given panel. But who enters the names, and who selects, among the many names proposed by the computer, the few who will serve at the center of the decision-making process, if not the program officer? Now there is the real power. If you control the levers of power at that crucial point, you already will have decided everything else—even if you do not know what is to be decided.

That is why it seems to me that the public interest would be well served if the composition of the panels were subject to systematic and ongoing scrutiny on the part of professional scholars. These should be people who represent the diverse viewpoints and trends in their fields, who have accomplished important scholarly exercises (for some programs) or who face significant scholarly challenges (for some) or who have distinguished themselves, even early in their careers, as teachers (for still others).

The community of academic humanists has a special, vested interest in two programs of the Endowment: Fellowships and Research. The composition of panels for fellowships, in particular, is simply critical. There are so many applicants (4,000 of the annual in-flow of 8,000 applications to the whole Endowment) that no one is able to master the entire corpus of materials and to exercise the requisite oversight. Yet no one individual, however experienced and efficient, can be expected to master all those detailed and substantive issues of professional learning in the humanities as to know whose judgment is to be trusted, and who is a bigot (of academic things).

No program officer can be asked to learn about the intricacies of the diverse and many fields deemed humanistic, from anthropology to musicology, history of all times and places, literature of everywhere, languages unlimited. But in nearly all fields addressed by the NEH flourish learned societies, small and large. These societies can and do supply the expert counsel of acknowledged leaders, people of learning, taste, judgment, restraint, and a sense of fairness. In my view we should turn to the learned societies to review the composition of the panels, to propose an ongoing flow of names for suitable candidates for inclusion in the process of reviewing applications and panel-discussion of them, and to share in the review and oversight (which are the work of the National Council on the Humanities) of the public and open disposition of public funds for humanistic purposes.

In this same context we come to the matter of an appeal or review procedure. It is no news that not every applicant comes away satisfied with the result of the process of review and adjudication of applications. Ours is not an entitlement program. Merely meeting the requirements guarantees nothing. Now if you do not succeed in applying for a fellowship or for research support, what are you supposed to do? If you write to the Endowment, you will (now) receive a full account of the reasoning of the panelists. If, from that point, you wish to appeal on grounds that (for example) that reasoning is false, or a lifelong enemy of yours clearly has sat on the panel (and the names are now released and made public), to whom do you appeal? The answer is, to the program officer who made up the panel to begin with.

It is a considerable burden on the program officer to confront the unhappy applicant, when the program officer bears full responsibility for the makeup of the panel which, to begin with, rejected the application. If professionals in the field have shared in the process of defining the panels, the appeal to expert knowledge is all the more credible. It can be made to stick. In this regard, Julie Motz proposes:

> That is why I suggest (1) that all applications in a given program be judged by the same set of specialists, and (2) these judges should be chosen from and by professional organizations in the field.

The role of the staff should be precisely what the staff now claims its role to be, namely, to serve the servants of the humanities, so to speak: to collect and dispose of applications, to call together an array of expert opinions, presented by people not chosen by staff (alone, or mainly) but chosen by experts in the diverse humanistic fields to begin with, and to hand on to the Council committee a full and fair account of what the experts have said.

The highly skilled and professional staff assembled in fifteen years of the Endowment's history is precisely as expert in its work as the scholars in the various humanistic fields are in theirs. Its work must then be so defined as to fall wholly within the actual experience and expert knowledge available to the member of the staff. The staff must not be asked to serve as clerks of a ministry of culture but as program officers of a Foundation, a great endowment for the humanities. For that is precisely what the National Endowment for the Humanities is meant to be, and I believe what the NEH truly is.

CHAPTER 5
NEH Occasions:
Open Meetings

The CIA cannot do its work in the open. The National Endowment for the Humanities, so far as it addresses the issues of humanistic learning and expression in this country, should not and cannot do its work behind closed doors. For the humanities demand public discourse, just as certain other forms of intelligence cannot endure it.

Even to precipitate public discussion of the National Council on the Humanities' need for secrecy, moreover, is to provoke debate on an issue which, to begin with, is not in the interest of the humanities. Such debate cannot secure for NEH that measure of good will and public understanding needed to lay the foundation for long-term public acceptance of the use of tax money for humanistic scholarship and activity. But doors are closed, so there must be debate.

Is it possible to imagine a well-constructed exercise in humanistic learning in which issues are not raised for inquiry? Is worthwhile inquiry conceivable when diverse viewpoints do not come to bear, when different modes of analysis are not applied? These are the substantial deeds we do when we practice the humanities as areas of learning and expression, and they are impossible other than in accord with the canons of discourse and criticism by which humanists live. That is why I find it incongruous to debate closing doors to the public discussion of public policy in the humanities, just as it is incongruous to conduct the work of intelligence out in the open.

Now the issue is not really phrased in these terms, for if it were, hardly anyone would find it worth much attention. But the issue is very much alive in the meetings of the National Council on the Humanities, the panel charged with oversight and review of Endowment activities. A tiny minority—often this writer alone—has taken the uncompromising position that, with a few special exceptions, when public policy about the use of public funds for humanistic projects comes under discussion, then meetings should be open. A continuing majority— often everybody else on the Council and in the senior administration of the Endowment—has maintained that, with a few exceptions, meetings should be closed.

No one argues that there are no grounds for closing Council meetings. When one citizen's opinions of another's proposal are at issue, discretion is demanded. But the Council's meetings rarely turn to specific applications at all. They deal in the main with matters of policy. At closed meetings in the past year, for example, several issues—deeply troubling to all humanists—have come up for discussion:

•continuing and permanent funding relationships between NEH and sizable humanities institutions which are transforming the Endowment, in effect, into an operating, or "regrant," agency and thus closing off possibilities for new programs;

• NEH contributions to endowment funds—for example, the ACLS—and the serious implications for the conversion of public funds into essentially non-public funds;

• decisions to spend more heavily on one field or topic than on some other—for example, American social history or women's studies; and

• the development of procedures for dealing with the appeals of disappointed applicants and policy regarding reconsideration of rejected applications.

These are fundamental issues. All of them have come before the Council, and NEH has made decisions with lasting implications for the humanities community in each case. Though I favor the administration's policy decisions on each matter, the fact that each is a basic issue of public policy—involving disposition of public funds and federal involvement in shaping the cultural life of this country—demands that the Council action be subject to public scrutiny.

And what should be scrutinized is the quality and character of the deliberation, the kinds of arguments adduced and analyses offered, as much as the actual decisions reached and the names of those on each side of a mooted point. Yet in the past year all of these matters have been discussed (and, I think, discussed thoughtfully), and in all instances decisions were reached without the presence of the press and public.

It is a privilege to serve on the Council, but it is also a responsibility. I am spending others' money, taxpayers' money. I expect to give reasons for my views and to justify my decisions. Scholars do that all the time. And humanistic scholars expect to be criticized and to learn from their critics.

How then can members of the National Council on the Humanities demand exemption from the exercise of those very modes of discourse and argument which, after all, humanists cherish, and which endow humanistic learning and expression with its particular gift of life? A humanities council that meets behind closed doors is a contradiction.

CHAPTER 6
NEH Occasions: The Humanities, Public Policy and Organized Jewry

The humanities are those areas of learning and expression which speak of who we are and what we can become as human beings. History traces beginnings; philosophy analyzes consciousness; literature records inner life and feelings; the study of religions turns to our highest aspirations. These and other subjects of "the sciences of humanity," as the humanities are called in France, or of "the science of the spirit," as the humanities are called in Germany, have one important distinction in America. It is the commitment of the nation, in its political and private institutions, to humanistic learning and expression, and the reciprocal concern of the humanities for public policy and the public interest. This interplay of learning and community is distinctive to America. It accounts for the remarkably high quality of cultural literacy in the country at large, measured, for instance, by museums, public TV and radio, and journalism.

What makes the Jewish community at home in the humanities is this same public commitment to learning, on the one side, and the dedication of learning to the community, on the other. There is nothing private or personal, let alone idiosyncratic, about learning in Judaism. Study in Judaism is a public act, rich in public consequences. That position is typical of Jewry through the ages: a basic tenet of Judaism is that learning is for everyone. But the engagement of the organized Jewish community in the humanities cannot depend only on a rather general conviction that learning matters. At stake is Jewish public policy, that is, a deeply American conviction about what we do together through organized action.

When we make sense of why the National Endowment for the Humanities is critical to the public interest, we shall also understand why programs of humanistic thought and expression are important to the institutions and organizations of American Jewry, indeed to those of all of the organized sectors of American social and cultural life. As I said, the public programs in the humanities brought into being through the National Endowment (1) celebrate and explore the sciences of humanities, the science of the spirit. They do so in such a way (2) as to enhance and enrich the national life. These are the two critical elements in the equation: the substance of the humanities, the purpose and relevance of the humanities to the public interest. One without the other lacks (1) either intellect, sensibility, and emotional value, or (2) pertinence and social value. But together these elements form a program and a promise for deepening our appreciation of ourselves, for understanding who we are and what we may become.

Stated very simply, in the formation of public policy the humanities contribute vision. They formulate, test, and criticize those propositions about purpose and definition, which all together add up to the directions and goals of society. So far as we see ourselves as a city on the hill and a model for the world, so far as we ask ourselves deep questions about what this country is "all about," we draw upon the whole of humanistic learning, history, philosophy, literature, the study of religions, and the other humane sciences. For fifteen years successive presidents and Congresses have affirmed that central task for the Endowment. They have supplied sizable funds, not freely given by donors but tax money. They have stated and restated conviction in these same propositions which I have tried to summarize.

What sustained and ongoing programs of humanistic learning and expression within the organized Jewish community can contribute must be discovered through analogy. For the organized community in its Federations and national organizations is a model, in America at large, for what voluntary action in the private, nonprofit sector of the common life is able to achieve. Strong countervailing institutions such as those created by Jewry not only serve the public good but preserve the possibility of choice in serving the public good. They do the work of society and do so not uniformly and coercively, as does government, but in diverse and multiple ways. They protect our regionalism in all of its dimensions. The importance *to* the humanities of the organized Jewish community and parallel structures is then clear: we know what can be done in government and in public programs. We are much less clear about what can be done through the nonprofit sector in the humanistic quest for vision and for learning. Labor unions, farm unions, ethnic groups of all kinds, come to the Endowment with effective proposals and produce first-rate humanistic programs. Yet there are effective institutions and organizations in this country, typified by the Jewish ones, which the Endowment has not yet succeeded in serving.

HUMANITIES, PUBLIC POLICY, ORGANIZED JEWRY 51

But the interest of the Jewish community (and its parallels) in joining forces with humanistic learning and expression has also to be explored. For we cannot take for granted that Jewry should undertake yet another layer of tasks, simply because it is in the public interest. The Jewish interest in the humanities, moreover, is to be explained not in general terms but in the context of the institutions and organizations which constitute the organized Jewish community. Jewry already maintains (if not entirely adequately) schools and colleges, libraries and research organizations, seminaries and yeshivas. These in fact as well as in form are institutions of the humanities. When we speak of public programs in the humanities within organized Jewry, we mean more than what there already is, that is to say, programs in Jewish education and institutions in Jewish culture. And, it is clear, we also mean more than higher appropriations within the budget of American Jewry for what Jews already have built in Jewish education and culture. We mean something fresh and unprecedented, and that is why we are here.

The reason the organized Jewish community will do well to explore the promise and prospect of humanistic learning and expression lies in the analogy of Jewry to the public at large. The substance of the Jewish humanities is an exercise in the exploration of Jewish definition and the explanation of Jewish purpose. The Jewish humanities—the study of the history, philosophy, literature, religion, and other creations and expressions of the inner world of the Jews, and the celebration and application of these Jewish humanities to the contemporary context of the American Jewish community—these modes of the sciences of humanity and the science of the spirit serve to celebrate ourselves. They generate vivid appreciation for who we have been and what we may become. What Jewry awaits, for the final decades of this century, is a vision of itself, a theory of its ongoing life, an account of what it is "all about." These things—the vision, the theory, the reason—must come from us all. They will emerge when we discover the humanist in ourselves. The humanities are the stimulus, the program, the discipline. For the organized Jewish community in search of itself, the Jewish humanities will serve to stimulate, to discipline, to bring freedom of imagination and breadth of emotion. In behalf of the humanities, I do not promise more than what the humanities in good measure have already done in the context of organizations and institutions throughout this country, under the auspices of the National Endowment for the Humanities.

What the Endowment contributes is not only the stimulus of federal funds. Money solves no problems all by itself. The Endowment has something more important to contribute. It is fifteen years of solid experience in public programs in the humanities. The NEH has written a record of achievement, of scrutiny of failure and success, an appreciation for our limitations, therefore a high estimation of our potentialities. Within its staff and administration, both here in Washington and also in the state councils on the humanities, are professionals of humanistic expression and activity, people with solid experience in guiding and evaluating practical programs. What makes these men and women truly professional, moreover, is their sense of their place and role, that is, their restraint, on the one side, and their pride in being able to serve and advise others, on the other.

It is one thing to speak of visions, theories, and goals. It is another to turn to those who have helped people *realize* their visions and assess their achievement in doing so. What the Endowment has to offer is its remarkable program, in all its variety and breadth of imagination, and its staff of people who have earned the title "public servants." The Endowment means to be the bridge between the national purpose which Congress and the President have assigned to it, on the one side, and the workaday life of the nation in all its amazing variety and inner power, on the other. Moving from humanistic insight to the concrete exercise and material application of that insight is the work of the Endowment. But it also is the work of all people who come together to organize themselves, to form a community.

Part II
Humanistic Approaches to Teaching About Judaism

CHAPTER 7
Contexts and Constituencies: The Diverse Responsibilities of Higher Jewish Learning

The development and rapid expansion of Jewish studies in undergraduate colleges and universities over the past two decades have created a new context and a fresh constituency for Jewish learning. The context is the liberal arts B.A., mainly in the humanities, in which knowing something about many things is deemed the goal. The constituency is the American undergraduate, Jewish but also gentile, drawn by (mere) curiosity, rewarded by insight, and, alas, more often than not, sustained by professors' instant wisdom. At the same time, these new developments have called for a reconsideration of existing contexts and constituencies. So what is now needed is a fresh asking of the question about (1) who teaches (2) what (3) to whom. For at the center of higher learning is the simple exercise of learning, in which one person teaches a given subject to some other: subject and predicate of accusative and dative. The context determines who teaches what. The constituency decides to whom. So these are critical issues of Jewish learning.

Thirty or forty years ago it was hardly necessary to raise them, because the answers were rightly deemed to be obvious. The constituency of Jewish learning was Jews, or some of them. The sole context was schools for training rabbis or teachers for the Jewish community. So the field was made up of Jews teaching Jewish subjects to Jews. There was no appreciable constituency of scholarship except for a few rabbis and unusual teachers. There were no important undergraduate or graduate programs in the major graduate centers of learning. That is not to say there were no important scholars at these centers, since everyone knows the record of Baron at Columbia and Wolfson at Harvard. But they did not systematically produce and place young scholars, and since, nowadays, a number of us do systematically produce and place young scholars, the difference is clear.

Now once we recognize that an important change has taken place, we confront a rather broad, if ignorant, range of assessments of that change, from those who maintain that nothing of importance for Jewish learning has taken place, to others who hold that a revolution has happened. In my judgment the question to be analyzed is not properly phrased when we ask whether everything or nothing has changed. We have on our hands a new context, which has taken its place (so to speak) alongside existing ones. We further have seen the development of a new constituency, again, alongside existing ones. Clearly much has changed. But to understand what has happened and is happening, we must reflect upon the entire context, the whole of the constituency of Jewish studies, paying attention to the old as well as to the new. Our question is how things now fit together, how they now work. In this setting, I may point out that some hold there is no need for Jewish institutions for Jewish learning, now that universities provide so ample and compendious a place for the subject. In the present context: Why do we need Dropsie University, if there are programs and departments of Jewish studies in universities? I shall deal with that question. To be sure, the same question is addressed to Jewish seminaries, teachers colleges, and various other types of contexts of higher Jewish studies, and in due course others will answer.

I

We may take up the matter precisely because we stand at the end of a period of rapid change and enter an age of stability in higher Jewish learning. Twenty years have passed since a fairly substantial number of appointments in Jewish studies came to fruition. The rate of growth is not what it was. Important institutions for Jewish studies, new journals, fresh monograph series, a broad program of conferences, annual meetings, exchanges of ideas, book reviewing, a variety of substantial graduate programs—the whole repertoire of a field of academic study at the height of its vigor and in the full bloom of its vitality now flourishes. Journals are read. Monographs are widely reviewed. The constituency for learning is sizable and solid. In the USA and Canada it soon will be time to assess how and whether the age of growth has produced significant learning, substantial in content, important and lasting in form.

The first principle and single most important criterion in my view is simple: each context—each type of program in higher Jewish learning—has its distinctive and important task. All of them together, the old and the new, must come under analysis. No setting for Jewish studies has yet proved to be superfluous. None is without its task. No constituency is to be ignored.

Whatever we have must be enhanced. Nothing must be lost, or there can be no gain at all. If the expansion of Jewish learning into universities leads some to suppose that there now should be a contraction outside of universities, then those people profoundly misunderstand the meaning of the new and misconstrue the value and the achievements of the established and enduring old. The various programs and institutions serve important constituencies, form significant and promising contexts for learning. We cannot concede any one of them to be superfluous or superannuated. What we must do is discover the strengths of each and discern how all fit together into a single and whole context, serving a diverse but essentially consistent (if not uniform) constituency.

II

There are four contexts for Jewish learning in America and Canada: (1) seminaries, (2) teachers colleges, and university programs of two distinct sorts, (3) the former, small programs, (4) the latter, large and sizable ones. There are many examples of small programs. As an instance that at Brown suffices, with three regular appointments (one in Tanakh, two in postbiblical Judaism), as well as a number of teaching assistantships for Hebrew and Talmud and a fair number of courses offered by specialists in other areas with expert knowledge in some area of Jewish learning, such as American Jewish literature, Jewish demography, political scientific work on the Jews, Zionism, and the like. The quantitative difference (small, large) becomes qualitative (a new context) when we compare our solid but modest program with the one at Brandeis, with sixteen full-time appointments in Judaic studies, numerous teaching assistantships, and the like. Brown represents one context, Brandeis a quite separate one, each with weaknesses and strengths. In this typology, Dropsie clearly belongs in the context of the large and free-standing program in Jewish studies. Since, moreover, Dropsie not only calls itself a university but also is entirely independent of theological or political commitments, it is to be located within the context of university-founded Jewish studies. If an important task is to be defined, Dropsie should be able to find it in the context of universities and serving the neutral constituency of college professors and students. In order to define such a context, we have to turn to the description and evaluation of that context and constituency framed by American and Canadian academic life.

In the neutral academic context of colleges and universities anyone who wants to may teach anything at all to whom it may concern. There is no focus, no center, and no clear-cut purpose, except as may be articulated within the local circumstance of a given department or university. I mean that we have no way of predicting what will be taught, of assessing the preparation and qualifications of the teacher, of explaining the place and importance of the subject in the education of the students, or of answering those other questions about curriculum and learning which, in general, make sense of learning. In so describing matters, of course, I describe not only the state of Jewish learning in universities, but also the state of university studies in general. The diversity and uneven character of higher education in America are accurately replicated in what is done in the small and unimportant field of Jewish studies. We call by a single name many different things. There is no predicting what a college or a university will be—for surely, the university which is Dropsie and the university which is Pennsylvania exhibit noteworthy differences and contrasts.

At the same time, because of the amplitude of positions, a further fact has to be noted. Most, though not all, Jewish scholarship in this country emerges from colleges and universities. That is a simple fact. It is proved to be a fact by reference to the other, equally simple, facts: Who writes the articles and books? Who reviews them? Who gives papers at meetings of learned societies, of a regional or national character? Who attends those papers and participates in the discussion of them? These are simple measures, requiring neither judgment nor approval. The bulk of Jewish learning in this country is the work of professors in colleges and universities. It is not the work of professors in Hebrew teachers colleges, who, except for a few individuals, produce very little. It is not the work of professors in yeshivas, who express their ideas in an academic idiom to which the stated criteria are irrelevant. It is in the main not the work of professors of Jewish seminaries, who, with exceptions, tend to see as their colleagues and students rabbis in the pulpits, rather than other professors in colleges and universities. The paramount reference-group and professional society for Jewish Theological Seminary of America professors tends to be the Rabbinical Assembly, for it is the agendum before the RA which occupies their time and attention, as the matter of ordaining women to be rabbis indicates. The same tends to be true for professors at Hebrew Union College-Jewish Institute of Religion and the Central Conference of American Rabbis, for it is there, more than at academic societies, that those colleagues tend to prefer to give their academic presentations, and in the journal of the rabbis that they write a fair number of their articles. The others find their way, mainly but not exclusively, into their house-journal—a very good one to be sure—the

Hebrew Union College Annual, refereed by themselves. The result is that they tend to talk mainly to one another about a common agendum and within agreed upon limits of discourse.

In general, therefore, with noteworthy exceptions (some at Hebrew Union College in Cincinnati, fewer at JTSA) the bulk of Jewish scholarly activity—measured solely by concrete achievement—in America and Canada takes place in the context of universities. I suppose that fact too should not be surprising, since for the humanities, nearly all serious learning in this country emerges from universities. If we take the narrower, but more appropriate, measure of scholarship in religious studies, it would appear to be that the bulk of scholarly achievement, but by no means all of it, is to be located in university departments of religious studies or in university divinity schools. We have then to ask ourselves why that should be the case.

To answer that question, we turn for the explanation of why American economists dominate the field of economics and receive the larger proportion of Nobel prizes in that field. The reasons, Gardner Ackly writes, are as follows:

> America's total population of trained economists is so much larger than any other that here there can be and are a great many trained and competent scholars, interested in every aspect of the subject. *They interact, criticize, evaluate, and stimulate each other and their graduate students, within and among campuses and research institutes, through journals, seminars, the exchange of working papers, and incessant shop talk.* [Italics supplied.]

What is characteristic of economics applies also to the humanities in general, and to the Jewish sector of the humanities in particular.

In universities we enjoy the stimulation of constant challenge. We are challenged to explain what we do in language accessible to people outside our field. This is stimulating, because it forces us to ask ourselves fundamental questions all the time. We are challenged to take up questions of common interest, and to answer those questions out of the data of Jewish experience and insight, which none concedes to be parochial. We are challenged to address ourselves to a sizable and complex agendum of learning coming to us from not only other specific fields of humanistic learning, but also theorists of humanistic learning in general. The humanities in America for the past thirty years have enjoyed a renaissance of learning. Important ideas, stimulating questions, stunning problems for inquiry, new modes of analysis and interpretation come out of our own universities as well as European ones. To be sure, American scholars are the persistent brides of Western learning, always in search of something new, something old, something borrowed—if not something blue. The new is always with us. We are experts *à la mode*. The old to us seems fresh. It is our naiveté to invent the wheel every day. We borrow like magpies ideas from everywhere. And, if truth be told, surrounded as we are by people of vitality and insight, we cannot become bored, self-absorbed, uninterested, or, therefore, the academic equivalent of blue.

So in universities there is a large critical mass of academic workers in Jewish learning. Their education in secular graduate programs and their professional context are broad and stimulating. They are not narrow in their interests. They constantly are with one another, by phone, at meetings, by letter, and in journals. They also are with people in other areas of learning adjacent, and by no means merely tangential, to theirs. There is constant shop talk. We teach one another. We criticize one another. We provoke one another. And the measurable results stand for all to see: in the journals in our field, and the disciplinary journals in other fields to which we contribute; on programs of the learned societies in our own field, and the learned societies in other fields and disciplines in which we take an active part; through the monographs and books we address to colleagues in our own field, and those we write for colleagues in a variety of fields; in the books we read and review. Truly it is an age of remarkable vitality. And the age, so far as Jewish learning is concerned, presently belongs mainly to universities.

Whether the reason that the faculties of Hebrew teachers colleges and seminaries tend to prove bored and boring, less productive than those in universities, is the inbred character of the faculties I do not know. It is a fact that most of the professors at the Jewish theological institutions are rabbinical and even doctoral graduates of those same institutions. Only a few of them have even taught elsewhere. As I said, it is commonplace for those professors to attend and to speak at the rabbinical meetings of the graduates of these schools. It is much less commonplace for them to speak at, or even attend, meetings of professors in their fields. Anyone who has attended the public sessions of the American Academy for Jewish Research must wonder at the absence of the collectivity of Jewish scholars employed by Jewish institutions—seminaries, teachers colleges. The Association for Jewish Studies' annual meeting attracts negligible numbers of professors of rabbinical schools and fewer still from teachers colleges. The program features their participation in disproportionately small numbers. So, in all, when the people stay home and see only one another, I suppose, they find so much about which to agree that stimulus is lacking to set out to do fresh work. Why take risks at all? Perhaps the absence of a grain of sand in the impenetrably hard and tightly closed shells of the

Jewish schools accounts for the difficulty we have in finding pearls. But it is a fact that not many rabbinical oysters yield pearls of great price, at least relative to the size of the oyster bed.

III

If we wish to discover where we are weak, we had best look closely at where we are strong. The strength of the university setting lies in its diversity and rich sources of intellectual stimulation. The weakness is in that same place: the diffusion of the field of Jewish studies across the curriculum—just as it should be; the negligible numbers of professors of Jewish studies in any one place, just as is the case in other small fields; the absence of a generally accepted standard of learning, so that professors of anything who happen to be born Jewish speak as equals to professors who have devoted their lives to the study of Judaica. The result is that courses tend to take shape around a totally unpredictable program. That is to say, as I said earlier, in universities anyone teaches anything to whom it may concern and calls it "Jewish studies."

We not only find a diversity of standards. We also discover no consensus that there are standards at all. People in general do not wish to submit their educational work, their curricula and their programs and course syllabi, to the criticism and review of colleagues. Nor do they wish to learn from colleagues' ideas about teaching. In this regard, I believe, we at Brown, patiently publishing our syllabi and not only sharing them but soliciting (and sometimes getting) the comments and judgments of colleagues, are alone. In general what is taught is a closely guarded secret.

Now it may be an open secret. For one instance, nearly every college has a "Holocaust" course, and everyone is supposed to know what to "do" in such a course. The fact that the study of the extermination of European Jewry has reached a high level of solid learning and professional scholarship does not deter colleagues who specialize in anything but that tragic era to teach "the Holocaust," as mainly fiction and theology. This too can mean anything from what really happened to what people feel about what happened, and, it goes without saying, among the hobbyists the appeal of novels and cheap theology is irresistible. To take another example, for the generality of teachers in language and literature courses, a course consists of the title of a book or a tractate. What one "teaches" is that book or tractate—chapter by chapter, line by line, so-called "exegetical method." So, the framer of the syllabus of the course is the one who wrote the book or redacted the tractate. Now that framer is hardly apt to be an educator. The redactor of a tractate is not one who has thought through what someone is supposed to learn in his tractate, why one should learn it in this way and order and not in some other way and order, and what the student will derive as benefit from the tractate. These are not the relevant issues. Books are not written by people who ask such educational questions.

But if teachers of language and literature abdicate the labor of thinking through the purpose and structure of their courses, teachers of history assume that their work is to say what came first and what happened then. Consequently, the syllabus of a course in history, in general, will be provided by someone's conception of the sequence and order of events. It is as if the principal point requiring explanation were why things happened in some given order, and it is as if the answer to the question were that they happened in that order, and so that is what they mean. I do not intend a caricature, but it is difficult to find an other-than-chronological principal of organization in the teaching of Jewish history. (Still, chronology is a step beyond the apologetics of "blood and peoplehood" which students get as "history" before they reach university studies.) In religious studies Jewish theological categories are supplied by the commonality of theology and filled with the detritus of rabbinical quotations out of context, wise sayings lacking all social relevance. So, overall, the scholarly vitality of the field masks something quite different: an intellectual vacancy, running hither-and-yon in search of what is in style. Jewish studies in universities reveal the absence of a clear-cut program by which the field unfolds, in accord with which a given subject is made into a course and is set into juxtaposition, and relationship, with some other course or courses, both in Judaic studies and in the disciplinary curriculum.

In fact we confront a field in search of itself. That is a mark of weakness, but also, as I said earlier, of strength. Diversity is strength; diffuseness, weakness. Response to rich stimulus makes our lives interesting; running in all directions all at once marks our intellectual life as trivial and modish. What is needed is a center of gravity, a source for order and intellectual community, a vehicle for educational stability. Now what I have said about Jewish studies in universities is not to be said about Jewish studies in Hebrew teachers colleges and Jewish seminaries. There there is an accepted and worthwhile curriculum. There is a stable and solid program of learning. People do emerge, in general, predictably literate in some subjects, in accord with a reasonable standard of learning. They do know some few things even very well: Hebrew language, Jewish texts of a classic and modern origin—things which fit together. By contrast to the niggardly smattering of facts and the excess of easy insight with which we equip our undergraduates, the students who complete the programs in the better Hebrew colleges and the more important seminaries and yeshivot do know both that they know some few things, and also that they do not know many other things.

For in knowing a few things well, they understand what knowing is, as our undergraduates do not. We who devote our lives to university studies of Jewish subjects have much for which to be proud: we have confronted a new context in a generally responsible and responsive way. We have not taken for granted that we know what is needed, which is pretty much what is done in Jewish contexts for Jewish studies. We have listened and tried to learn about the unprecedented context presented by powerful institutions of general culture to which, for the first time in history, Jewish learning finds its way. We have taken seriously the unprecedented requirements of a wholly new setting for Jewish learning. We have made full use of the intellectual opportunities of our day.

But for this we shall be called to account: for educating a generation of young Jews and gentiles to think that it is much easier to enter into the disciplines of Jewish learning than it actually is. For that, and for one more thing: in all too many instances, for not educating at all but calling the result learning.

IV

In my judgment the lamentable traits of Jewish studies in universities outlined just now define one useful and important program of work for a school such as Dropsie University (or Brandeis University). I refer now to those types of institutions with large faculties and a paramount commitment to Jewish learning, and yet also with freedom of vision and exemption from partisan and apologetic commitment so that truly humanistic, interesting learning is possible. What is needed, specifically, is a faculty of true scholarly achievement, capable of serving as a source for broadening and deepening the learning of the scholars in colleges and universities. I refer to creating a center for Jewish humanistic studies meant to serve, in particular, the overburdened professors of Jewish this, that, and the other thing, in the colleges and universities of the country. It would be a postgraduate center for broadening knowledge of some few things, and for deepening knowledge of some one thing. What is needed, in particular, is a place for use for sabbaticals, a center for advanced study of a rather particular order. Let me unpack this rather simple idea.

If there were no Dropsie University, perhaps, in this day and age, no one would think of creating it. But there is such a place. Its leadership does seek an important and critical task in American higher education. After a long period in which it lay moribund, Dropsie now takes up a new set of tasks, enters a new period in its own history. I salute that ambition. I cherish that fresh hope. I wish to encourage the dream of renewal and rebirth. For, as I said earlier, we must prize whatever we now have, lose nothing, but reform and renew everything. Every student, every institution, every professorship, every library and librarian, all faculties and administrations, even the bricks in the handful of buildings devoted to Jewish learning—these are all we have. They are the blood and bone of whatever intellectual and scholarly life American Jewry is going to have in our day. There is not apt to be much more than what we now have. But we can see that there will not be less.

To carry the argument forward, one important task I see for Dropsie is to frame a program (among its other programs, to be sure) for postdoctoral studies here in Philadelphia, with its remarkable Jewish intellectual resources, its universities and Jewish institutions. Such a center should provide residential fellowships for both senior scholars and junior ones. It should be conceived along the lines of the National Humanities Center in North Carolina and the various other centers for humanistic and scientific study in this country. These are places in which scholars are brought together for a year of common discourse and study. The result of a year of such study is that professors work together with professors, younger with older, accomplished people with beginners; in all a community of learning takes shape and begins to flourish.

Such centers for humanistic study are not merely places in which individuals pursue their personal research interests or ask questions of more learned people while they engage in private projects. On the contrary, that kind of essentially individual work does not require the locus of a center at all. What centers offer which individual studies do not is the formation of a timely community of people who wish to talk together and work together over a protracted period. These people have the time and energy and will to learn how to converse with and learn from one another. They are scholars who appreciate how individual labors must benefit, must be fructified, in a community of learning.

If such a center is to make its contribution to the stabilization of Jewish studies in universities, it must also make provision to continue the education of the professors themselves. For, as I indicated earlier, in the nature of our work all of us are called upon to teach many more things than we have studied. Without fear of contradiction by other equally informed people, we express our opinions about anything we like. In our area of work, we reign supreme but also alone, monarchs of a realm consisting, in the main, of not much more than ourselves. The result, as is clear, is that we opine about too much, and we take our measure too little. A program of systematic studies in fields we teach but have not studied is as important as a research colloquium. The particular nature of the field demands that we broaden ourselves, so as to become better informed teachers to our undergraduates.

Dropsie can turn itself into something we do not now have and do need: a center for Jewish studies in universities. To Dropsie the people who do the work in universities may retreat for renewal, for intellectual encounter with peers, for fresh exercises in systematic learning. For that purpose, what is needed are two sorts of professors. First is a resident corps of teachers for some of the disciplines and subjects required, yet not widely mastered, in universities. Second is a revolving corps of teachers and students for the successive research colloquia to be organized over the years. These two programs, one in systematic study, the other in collective research on important and shared problems, will attract to Dropsie the people who today do the work, who actually meet the educational payroll so to speak. We who bear the full responsibility, but also the full power, for the character of Jewish studies in universities wind to such an initiative. The labor of integrating the field, of providing it with a critical and vital center, of nurturing a common discourse about standards of teaching, the character of useful curricula, and a shared program of education and even of culture—that labor seems to me worthy of the resources at present subjected to the careful inspection of thoughtful and ambitious people.

What is needed is a center of gravity, a source for order and intellectual community. For the Hebrew colleges and seminaries, the established tradition of learning forms such a center and such a source. It is a tradition of a given order for a given purpose. That tradition explains why, in those places, people do things in one way and not in some other. Rabbinical schools have a pretty clear idea of what they think rabbinical students should study. Hebrew colleges have a fairly standard definition for the subjects their students should learn. But we in universities and colleges do not. It is clear that our distinctive context is not going to, and ought not, provide us with a focus and center of gravity congruent to the tradition of learning of Jewish studies which is our subject.

V

So now the question is raised: With the various Judaic studies programs in universities, is Dropsie University still needed? I believe I have given one answer to the question. This is an answer relevant to the field of Jewish learning as a whole. If you want to know how Dropsie may find a place in the very center and heart of the vast enterprise of Jewish learning in this country and Canada, then seek the flaw at the center, the ache at the heart, of our common corpus of studies.

There is a university constituency to be served. It is made up of scholars of Jewish studies as well as scholars of other subjects with special knowledge and competence in Jewish studies of a more narrow order. There is a major task to be done to take both of these types of scholars and improve their capacities to pursue learning and education in universities. It is not a task which is apt to be done in any other institution. Universities in general are not likely to deem Jewish studies so critical within the larger curriculum as to warrant the effort and investment required for the formation of a residential center for the Jewish humanities. Jewish seminaries and teachers colleges do not have the intellectual resources, the vision, or the understanding of context to form such a center. That is because they are essentially removed from the life and problems of universities and do not grasp (or care to grasp) what these are.

Consequently, I perceive a special labor for which Dropsie may make itself especially qualified. Professor David Goldenberg writes to me, "I happen to think that the potential is here for a leading center of Judaic studies in America, because it is the only institution exclusively devoted to the subject and yet nontheological." I concur in this judgment. That is why I offer for consideration this theory of a problem and how Dropsie may choose to meet it.

To conclude: the constituency is the vast body of American college students who take our courses. The context is the study of Jewish subjects in universities. But the meeting of context and constituency has now to take place in yet another place, on yet another plane. Whether or not Dropsie constitutes the right place, whether or not this is the right time, and whether or not the lay leaders and president and professors are the right people—these are questions to be settled by the people themselves. I should not have raised these questions if I thought no response might come forth. The question is whether this is the time and the place for a national residential center for postdoctoral humanistic Judaic studies. I do not know the answer. But I do know that, if it is not here, it is not apt to be elsewhere either.

CHAPTER 8
Contexts and Curricula: Introducing Judaism in the Humanities. The First Course and its Problems

I. *The Elementary Course*

An introductory course in a university, strictly speaking, is any course which has no prerequisite. Since, in the humanities (excluding language studies), it is unusual to require a prerequisite, most courses in fact introduce not only the subject but also the discipline. This is so without regard to the location of the course within the program of studies, that is, whether it is deemed for beginners or for advanced students, whether it bears a low or a high number. And, it must be said, even courses for which a student must qualify by taking a prior subject in fact impose few demands; the instructor's permission commonly replaces that prior course. So, in all, for the humanities, most of what we do is to introduce some part of the subject we teach. Our work is perpetually elementary.

There are courses, nonetheless, which clearly address themselves to the fundamental issues of a subject or field. These serve to draw students to work in that field, on the one side, or to tell students pretty much all they will ever know about that field, on the other side. That is, they conventionally serve as the first experience of a student in the given subject, and, it is understood, they may also serve as the last. Or students may decide to take further courses in that field. In the former aspect these courses fall under the category of performing "service," in that students from many different departments may elect them, and, in the latter, they take their place as part of the "major."

It is the ambiguity of such courses and their clientele which makes teaching them especially interesting. We have to speak with many voices, portray our subject with multiple vision, address the most private issues and those accessible to our discipline and its modes of discourse, all at once.

There is a taxonomy of such courses to be specified. One type of introductory course presents the rudiments of a discipline, for example, explains the several methods used in the academic study of religions. A second type, which is quite distinct, presents the fundamental facts of a given religion, or of a given phenomenon affecting diverse religions, e.g., Judaism, or the nature of religious society. In this type, the methods used in the course may not be made explicit, but, since data never speak for themselves but are given a voice by one method or another, methods once more require explication. A third type introduces the subject, "religion," or delineates the subject by some distinctive trait, for instance, "Catholicism-Protestantism-Judaism," or "the religions of the West," or "the religions of the Orient." This is a variation on the second type. What these three types of courses have in common is that they attempt to survey a vast range of material. The normal mode is to block and choose, that is, block out a wide range of data and choose, for careful study, some quite specific and concrete problem. This choice is to be suggestive for a wider range of issues.

A quite distinct kind of introductory course will present a much smaller topic or problem than "Judaism" or "Methods in the Study of Religions" or "The Religions of the West" or "Religion and Society." It takes up instead a very narrow theme, such as "American Judaism" or "Zen Buddhism" or "Medieval Christianity." Now as soon as I give these topics, the reader will have wondered how one may characterize them as "narrow"; yet, compared to the earlier ones, they clearly represent another, and more limited, sort of course entirely. Yet, I maintain, these too in fact constitute introductory courses, so long as students are not required to elect antecedent ones on that very subject, e.g., "Religions in America" before "American Judaism," or "Medieval History" before "Medieval Christianity," or "Judaism in Europe" before "American Judaism." If a course does not directly relate to the materials of its successor, that is, of the course which it serves as prerequisite, then the successor-course is not an advanced course in any material sense. Since students begin the subject, the course introduces that subject. True, a "methods-course" will define how we approach a given subject. But it will not provide the student with knowledge of that subject, and, therefore, as I said, the course which does provide the elementary facts and undertakes their preliminary interpretation must be deemed introductory.

I argue this proposition with some care so that the repertoire of suitable subjects for introductory courses on Judaism may be broadened. There is no reason that we should assume we know just what must be done for an introduction, that is, describe the "beliefs and practices of Judaism," or assume there is a normative course of some one kind, e.g., a history of the Jews or a history of Judaism. There is no limit to the range of topics and problems upon which we may draw for our introductory course, except our own imagination and academic conscience. These are criteria for the exercise of our taste and judgment on what is to be introduced and how we propose to introduce our subject. First, we have limited time. So we must choose something important, with lasting intellectual consequences. Second, the students have little preparation for the subject. The gentile and Christian students have none, and their impressions are vague and vapid. The Jewish ones emerge from an educational system which, at best, imparts a smattering of Hebrew. But they have rich access to their own memories and experiences, and these require sorting out and examination. Since we do not propose to teach Judaism under a scheme of intellectual *apartheid*, with one course for Jews and another for others, we have to find a set of questions and issues relevant to, and within the grasp of, students of diverse character. Third, and still more important, in introducing our subject we have to take full account of its context, that is, academic work. It follows that what we teach should be continuous with other studies in the university and department (discipline) in which we teach, and not with the system of Jewish or Christian schools, of whatever character, out of which some of our students emerge. The social definition of our setting, therefore, is the university and its intellectual continuum. A student coming into a course on Judaism should not have reason to wonder whether, in this setting, he confronts essentially distinctive modes of thought, an agendum of learning fundamentally different from that which governs other courses in the humanities. These seem to me some of the important criteria in the decisions to be made on how to teach introductory courses on Judaism in departments of religious studies.

By now it should be quite obvious that no one course may claim to exhaust the possibilities of introduction. Any course is a very small and concrete, but wholly practical, judgment upon elevated issues of the intellect. It is applied reason and practical and practiced learning. Each instructor, therefore, will make judgments and decisions. Of greater consequence, as we learn from what works and what does not work, and as our own tastes and ideas change, the character of our courses, even when they bear the same title, will change too. It is unthinkable to me that a course, even using pretty much the same textbooks and following the same sequence of themes and problems, will essentially replicate itself from one year to the next. Our courses are the expression of ourselves. If we repeat them unchanged from year to year, it means we either have made no mistakes, or have not learned from, or even recognized, the mistakes we have made.

These general observations will take on greater meaning when brought to bear upon several specific examples of introductory courses I have given. I offer my own work as an example not to be followed but to be explained and criticized. All we have to offer is experience, the concrete example of a theory followed at one time and dropped in favor of some other. Teaching is an art, at which no one can claim to excel all the time, or need to admit to constant failure either. To learn how to practice an art, all we are able to do is to see how others have practiced it, to learn from their errors, and perhaps to copy their successes and hope they work for us too. If I claim for myself any merit at all, it is merely the courage to admit in public to what I have done in my classroom, and to offer for the experiment and criticism of others the sorts of things which, over twenty years of teaching, I have come to think worthwhile.

II. *The Purpose of a Course-Syllabus*

What I present for analysis are the syllabi of a number of courses given over the past few years. The purpose of a course-syllabus should be specified. It is not merely a "bibliography." Unlike the practice in European and Israeli universities, we do not merely hand out lists of books and expect students to find their own way. Perhaps we should. But our educational tasks are distinctive and would not be well served in such a way. A syllabus in our hands specifies some things and signals others by indirection. It specifies where a student should be at a particular time, what books a student should possess, what pages in those books should be read for a given session. Students learn best when they know where they are in the unfolding of a subject, and they are (for good or ill) happiest when they know what is expected of them and believe they can meet those expectations. A syllabus is therefore essential, in our approach to teaching, to provide the students with a clear sense of the order and structure of a course (assuming the course is a well-planned and orderly exposition of its subject).

A syllabus serves a second purpose, however, and this is why it should be analyzed and carefully unpacked. It states a theory of the subject and makes decisive judgments about how the subject should unfold, what comes first and what comes second. So in all, it makes an emphatic statement of a theory of the logic of its subject. A course lacking a theory of the subject simply presents information, but no ideas and surely no insight. A course which teaches a subject in one way, and not in some other, because of a larger theory of the character and inner logic of the subject, will provide a measure of insight. For the ideal is for a student to see not merely the traits of the subject but how the subject works. Taking apart the theme of the course and seeing its inner parts—these are, in my judgment, the worthwhile modes of learning. Finally, a course which teaches a subject in such a way as to exemplify a larger problem or to point toward the greater potentialities and implications of this particular chapter of learning is the highest goal. That is when a university becomes worthy of its name: a place of discourse on many things, but from the perspective of encompassing reason. Occasionally I find myself able to teach a course on Judaism from which students learn something about the nature of religion. I may succeed in so shaping a subject as to illustrate a larger problem of interpretation, a larger scheme of knowledge. On those rare moments I should be prepared to claim success for my work. In the syllabi that follow, these goals are going to be detected principally in the introductory statements about the purpose of a course, in the headings of the several units of a course, and in the character of the reading which I assign.

One thing will become obvious at the outset. I have edited or written the majority of the books which I use in my elementary courses. The reason is that most of these books are anthologies, with the opinions of many different scholars amply represented. I brought them into being for diverse kinds of courses which I teach. A very few of them are wholly under my authorship and speak out of my own scholarly work. I regard it as a responsibility of scholars to address students with a clear and accessible account of the main, and usable, results of disciplined learning. This I have done. A few of them are out-and-out textbooks, in which I provide what I conceive to be a coherent account of the subject mainly in my own words, not as an anthology, and also not as an account of my own scholarly work. These generally serve to provide a framework for my larger pedagogical work. To assess the courses outlined here, it may be necessary to consult the specific readings assigned in the several anthologies. Otherwise the shape and structure of the readings will hardly be clear.

In recent years I have made fairly extensive use of movies. Very belatedly I have noticed that students learn effectively through what they see and hear, because they are raised on television. Instead of bemoaning that self-evident fact, I have decided to try to make use of it. The main educational task is to use the various movies to exemplify important problems, to allow the students to derive both information and understanding from what they see. This requires not only the showing of movies but, obviously, discussion of what one is to look for before the movies and analysis of what one has seen afterward. It is principally for the modern phase of the history of Judaism that movies are useful as primary sources. I tend to look for different ones from one year to the next, mainly because I find it dull to see ones I have already seen. But there are types of movies which remain the same, and for certain units, these types will prove useful every year.

One type of movie must help the students see the shift in the role and aspirations of women in Judaism, which I regard as a critical subject for contemporary study. For this purpose *Hester Street* is exceedingly effective, and *I Love You, Rosa* may serve as well. There are numerous effective movies on the destruction of European Jewry, and one valuable exercise is to analyze the different viewpoints of the moviemakers upon the common subject under discussion. *The Eighty-First Blow*, for example, proves to yield nearly as much insight about the operative civil religion of the State of Israel as it does about the events of 1933 to 1945. The reader will notice that I invariably cancel class on the day of a movie. The reason is that I want the student to take the movie seriously and to regard it as integral to the work of the course. I also advertise the movie so that people in the university and community feel free to come.

III. *A Chronological Introduction to the History of Judaism*

The first course for consideration is the most conventional. It is an "introduction to Judaism" which introduces the subject along essentially historical and chronological lines. It outlines the several periods in the history of Judaism and describes the principal traits of the "Judaism" expressed in those periods. Since what emerges is a rather one-dimensional account of this and that, not a cogent picture of a religion, Judaism, I made the critical conceptual issue of the course the problem of defining Judaism out of the diverse data assembled along the way.

> The problem of this course is to define "Judaism," in particular to solve the dilemma of finding appropriate definition for a diverse and ancient religious tradition. The course consists of lectures and sections. Reading assignments, which average 100 pages a week, are to be completed by the section meeting at which they are to be discussed.

Introduction to the Course. The problem of defining a definition.
    Recommended: Neusner, *Understanding Rabbinic Judaism*, pp. 405–11.
       I. *The Biblical Foundation of Judaism*
         Neusner, *Way of Torah*, pp. 1–8.
         Kaufman, "The Biblical Age," in Schwarz, *Great Ages and Ideas of the Jewish people*, pp. 3–92.

CONTEXTS AND CURRICULA 73

      Spiegel, "Amos vs. Amaziah," in *Life of Torah*, pp. 31-40.
      Genesis 1-2
      The Book of Amos.
      The Book of Deuteronomy
II. *Varieties of Judaism before A.D. 70, Sectarian and Normative*
      Ralph Marcus, "The Hellenistic Age," in Schwarz, *Great Ages*, pp. 95-142.
      Geza Vermes, *The Dead Sea Scrolls in English*, pp. 11-68, 69-94, 149-68.
      Apocrypha: Ecclesiasticus: Jesus son of Sirach, Chapters 24, 35, 36, 38, 44-50.
      New Testament: Matthew, Romans 9-11, Galatians.
III. *Pharisaism before 70*
      Neusner, *From Politics to Piety: The Emergence of Pharisaic Judaism*, pp. 1-45, 81-154.
IV. *Rabbinic Judaism: Origins and Character*
      Neusner, *Way of Torah*, pp. 9-28.
      _____, *There We Sat Down: Talmudic Judaism in the Making*, pp. 19-140.
      _____, *Understanding Rabbinic Judaism*, pp. 11-23.
      Recommended: Gerson Cohen, "The Talmudic Age," in *Great Ages*, pp. 143-214.
V. *The Religious Life of (Rabbinic) Judaism*
      Neusner, *Life of Torah*, pp. 17-24, 81-150.
      Guttmann, "The Religious Ideas of Talmudic Judaism," in *Understanding Rabbinic Judaism*, pp. 37-52.
VI. *Philosophy, Mysticism, and Rabbinic Judaism*
      Abraham Halkin, "The Judeo-Islamic Age," in *Great Ages*, pp. 215-65.
      I. Twersky, "Maimonides," in *Understanding Rabbinic Judaism*, pp. 185-212.
      Neusner, *Way of Torah*, pp. 50-57.
      Gershom G. Scholem, "General Characteristics of Jewish Mysticism," in *Understanding Rabbinic Judaism*, pp. 243-76.
      Recommended: M. Kaplan, "Medieval Jewish Theology," in *Understanding Rabbinic Judaism*, pp. 133-46.
      Abraham J. Heschel, "The Mystical Element of Judaism," in *Understanding Rabbinic Judaism*, pp. 277-300.
VII. *Jews and Judaism in Modern Times*
      Salo Baron, "The Modern Age," in *Great Ages*, pp. 315-419.
      Neusner, *Way of Torah*, pp. 61-94.
      Louis Ginzberg, "Israel Salanter," in *Understanding Rabbinic Judaism*, pp. 353-82.
VIII. *American Judaism*
      Neusner, *American Judaism: Adventure in Modernity*, pp. vii-viii, 1-86, 143-54.
      Emanuel Rackman, "Orthodoxy"; Abraham J. Feldman and Jakob J. Petuchowski, "Reform Judaism"; and Theodore Friedman, "Conservative Judaism," in *Life of Torah*, pp. 155-83.
IX. *Contemporary Judaism and Zionism*
      Baron, "The Modern Age," in *Great Ages*, pp. 420-54.

Jack Nusan Porter and Peter Dreier, eds., *Jewish Radicalism*, pp. 1-50.
Neusner, *Life of Torah*, pp. 205-34.
X. *Conclusion*
Neusner, *Way of Torah*, pp. 95-99.
_____, *Life of Torah*, pp. 5-16.
Reading period assignment:
Neusner, *Invitation to the Talmud* (Harper & Row).

IV. *An Analytical Introduction to Systems of Judaism*

While the course outlined above proved interesting, it seemed to me a fresh approach would promise more useful insight. Specifically, I wanted to see whether, instead of simply outlining a sequence of "Judaisms" and asking whether it was possible to define "Judaism" out of the diverse data produced over the centuries, I might entirely eliminate the issue of historical chronology. What is important *about* "Essenism" or "Hasidism" or "Talmudic Judaism," after all, is not when these kinds of Judaism flourished, but, rather, *how* they worked. What is it that we learn from them which might prove helpful in the analysis of contemporary expressions of Judaism and of other religions? For that purpose, analysis of a *system* within Judaism, with due respect for its particular historical and social setting, seemed to me a preferable experiment. The opening paragraph spells out the problem.

The reader will notice that the page-assignments are considerably smaller than in the earlier course. As I learn more about teaching, I have come to prefer that the students read a smaller number of pages with great care, rather than a larger number in a rushed and often sloppy way. In the former sort of assignment lies the possibility of learning.

> This course explores the proposition that, at various points in history, the Jews have set forth distinct and distinctive "systems"—ways of living and world-views—which defined and explained the worlds in which they lived. Each of these systems, moreover, had to deal with certain constants, characteristic of the Jews as a group for the whole of their history. The course addresses three problems: (1) the description of some of the systems of Judaism (specifically: Biblical, Essene, Rabbinic, Zionist, Reform, and American), (2) the interpretation of these systems by reference to the world meant to be explained by them, and (3) the comparison of the several systems subject to description and interpretation.
>
> I. *Introduction to the Course*
> II. *Two Biblical Systems*
>   Read: The Book of Deuteronomy, The Book of Leviticus.

CONTEXTS AND CURRICULA

III. *The Essenes' System*
Read: Geza Vermes, *The Dead Sea Scrolls in English*, pp. 11-52, 69-148.

IV. *Out of the Holocaust: Formation of the Rabbinic System*
Read: Neusner, *Between Time and Eternity*, pp. 1-46.
_____, *Understanding Jewish Theology*, pp. 11-62.

V. *The Maturing of the Rabbinic System: Talmudic Judaism*
Read: Neusner, *There We Sat Down*, pp. ix-xx, 19-140.

VI. *Traits of (Rabbinic) Judaism*
Read: Neusner, *Between Time and Eternity*, pp. 47-114.
_____, *Understanding Jewish Theology*, pp. 89-148.

VII. *The Crisis of Modernity: Tradition and Change*
Movie, to be shown at 7:30 p.m., Carmichael Auditorium, I LOVE YOU, ROSA.
This is instead of a class session.
Read: Neusner, *Between Time and Eternity*, pp. 115-30.
_____, ed., *Understanding Jewish Theology*, pp. 229-70.
_____, *American Judaism: Adventure in Modernity*, pp. 1-13.

VIII. *Theological Systems and Modernization: Reform Judaism*
Read: Neusner, ed., *Understanding Jewish Theology*, pp. 149-64, 196-214, 259-70.
_____, *Between Time and Eternity*, pp. 130-45.
_____, *American Judaism: Adventure in Modernity*, pp. 117-42.

IX. *Assimilationism as a System of Judaism*
Movie, to be shown at 7:30 p.m., List 120, THE JAZZ SINGER.
This is instead of a class session.
Read: Philip Roth, *Portnoy's Complaint*.
Neusner, *American Judaism: Adventure in Modernity*, pp. 61-86.

X. *Zionism as a System of Judaism*
Class lecture: David Goodblatt, University of Haifa.
Read: Neusner, *Between Time and Eternity*, pp. 145-54.
_____, *Understanding Jewish Theology*, pp. 73-88.
_____, *American Judaism: Adventure in Modernity*, pp. 87-116.

XI. *The "Holocaust" and Judaism*
Movie, to be shown at 7:30 p.m., Carmichael Auditorium, NIGHT AND FOG, GENOCIDE.
Read: Neusner, *Understanding Jewish Theology*, pp. 163-94.
_____, *Between Time and Eternity*, pp. 154-66.
Elie Wiesel, *Gates of the Forest*.

XII. *American Judaism*
Read: Neusner, *Between Time and Eternity*, pp. 166-76.
_____, *American Judaism: Adventure in Modernity*, pp. ix-xx, 15-3 35-60, 143-54.

FINAL: You will be asked to describe two or three "systems" in the history of Judaism, to compare them to one another, and to evaluate each in terms of the ongoing tasks of any system put forward out of Judaism. The final must be typed. It may go from 10 to 15 pages, but no longer than that. The work of systematic analysis, not description, is at the center of the assignment.

V. *A Particular Topic: (1) American Judaism*

It should not be thought that the only kind of introductory course is one which tells the whole story, from beginning to end, of the history and structure of Judaism. Another kind of elementary or "first course" is one which takes a specific topic and raises questions in the analysis of that topic. The results of this analysis will, in due course, serve for the study of quite fresh themes. A fair exemplification of this kind of course is one on American Judaism, a very attractive subject for our students because nearly all of them have studied American history and most of them have some impressions of, or even experience with, Judaism as it is formulated in this country and in Canada. The readings in the anthologies, *Understanding American Judaism*, are quite diverse and introduce a wide variety of movements and viewpoints.

> The purpose of this course is to analyze and interpret the nature of religion in modern and contemporary times, using Judaism in America as the specimen. What does it mean to "be religious"? What are the ambiguities of religiosity? What does it mean not to "be religious"? What are the complexities of secularity? How does inherited religious culture change and, at the same time, affect the nature of change? These questions intersect with another set: What is American about American Judaism? What is Judaic, carrying forward abiding phenomena of classical or Rabbinic Judaism? And there is yet a third set of questions: What is the meaning of "Jewishness," the ethnic, professedly non-religious congeries of social and cultural traits emergent in contemporary American Jewish life?

    I. *Asking the Question*
       Neusner, *American Judaism: Adventure in Modernity*, pp. vii–viii, 1–3, 143–53.
       _____, *Understanding American Judaism*, I, pp. xvii–xxv, 3–65; II, 303–26.
       Chapman, *Jewish-American Literature*, pp. 279–99.
    II. *Uprooting and Replanting*
       Neusner, *American Judaism: Adventure in Modernity*, pp. 4–9.
       Glazer, *American Judaism*, pp. 12–78.
       Handlin, *The Uprooted*, pp. 7–57, 85–104.
       Chapman, *Jewish-American Literature*, pp. 238–53.
    III. *First Fruits: Children and Grandchildren*
       Nathan Glazer, *American Judaism*, pp. 79–129.
       Oscar Handlin, *The Uprooted*, pp. 105–269.

CONTEXTS AND CURRICULA 77

        Chapman, *Jewish-American Literature*, pp. 193–207, 37–45, 307–309, 569–86.
- IV. *American Judaism as Religion: 1. The Rabbi*
        Neusner, *American Judaism: Adventure in Modernity*, pp. 35–60.
        ———, *Understanding American Judaism*, I, pp. 103–14, 141–215.
- V. *Amerian Judaism as Religion: 2. Reform and Conservative Judaism*
        Neusner, *Understanding American Judaism*, II, pp. 3–104, 195–218, 247–302.
- VI. *American Judaism as Religion: 3. Orthodoxy*
        Neusner, *Understanding American Judaism*, I, pp. 269–84; II, pp. 105–94.
- VII. *The "American Jewish Way of Life"*
        Neusner, *American Judaism: Adventure in Modernity*, pp. 9–13, 15–34, 61–85.
        ———, *Understanding American Judaism*, I, pp. 69–101.
        Marshall Sklare, *America's Jews*, pp. 103–54.
- VIII. *Modes of "Jewishness": 1. Culture*
        Philip Roth, *Goodbye Columbus*.
        Chapman, *Jewish-American Literature*, pp. 694–727, 654–64, 346–50, 387–406.
- IX. *Modes of "Jewishness": 2. Zionism, Israelism*
        Neusner, *American Judaism: Adventure in Modernity*, pp. 87–116.
        Porter and Dreier, *Jewish Radicalism*, pp. 51–118.
        Sklare, *America's Jews*, pp. 210–23.
        Chapman, *Jewish-American Literature*, pp. 546–59.
- X. *Modes of "Jewishness": 3. Radical Jewishness, New Jews, Women*
        Nathan Glazer, *American Judaism*, pp. 151–86.
        Porter and Dreier, *Jewish Radicalism*, pp. 1–50, 149–78, 243–72.

Suggestions for reading period assignment:
The immigrant experience:
        Moses Rischin, *The Promised City. New York's Jews, 1870–1914*.
        Mark Zborowski and Elizabeth Herzog, *Life Is with People*.
The history of American Jews:
        Henry L. Feingold, *Zion in America*.
        Oscar Handlin, *Adventure in Freedom*.
Zionism and American Jews:
        Melvin I. Urofsky, *American Zionism from Herzl to the Holocaust*.
American Jewish Literature:
        Allen Guttman, *The Jewish Writer in America: Assimilation and the Crisis of Identity*.
A novel of American Judaism:
        Ludwig Lewisohn, *The Island Within*.
A theological novel:
        Arthur A. Cohen, *In the Days of Simon Stern*.
Some American Judaic theologians and theologies:
        Richard L. Rubenstein, *After Auschwitz*.
        Mordecai M. Kaplan, *The Future of the American Jew*.
        Herman Wouk, *This Is My God*.
        Alan W. Miller, *The God of Daniel S. In Search of the American Jew*.

Milton Steinberg, *A Partisan Guide to the Jewish Problem.* "Radical Jewishness," etc.
J. Neusner, ed., *Contemporary Judaic Fellowship. In Theory and in Practice.*

VI. *A Particular Topic: (II) Zionism*

Yet another introductory course takes up not a conventional phenomenon of Judaism, such as American Judaism, but rather a single movement. For this purpose I select one of two movements which have reached their full promise both in theory (theology, ideology) and in social expression and institutional potentiality: Reform Judaism and Zionism. Zionism is much easier to teach, because of the cogency of its theoretical issues and because of the clear-cut beginning, middle and end, which, in the nature of things, the movement exhibits. In the past I have tended to end the course in 1948. In the present version I have chosen to devote a good deal of attention to Zionism in America and, more especially, to the Zionist analysis of American Jewry and of American Judaism.

> This course explores the diverse theoretical systems which, before 1948, reached the conclusion that the Jews should create a Jewish state, and which further explored the character of that state after it would be brought into being, the politics required to accomplish that goal, the definition of the meaning of "being Jewish" created in the light of that goal, and the diverse other powerful intellectual forces subsumed under the movement of Zionism. The stress is on the interplay between political and social theory, on the one side, and the political and social realities of the Jewish people, on the other.

I. *The Formation of Zionist Theory*
  Introduction to the Course
   Hertzberg, *The Zionist Idea*, pp. 14-100.
  Zionism in the Nineteenth Century
   Howard Sachar, *A History of Israel*, pp. 3-36.
   Hertzberg, pp. 116-40, 178-98.
  Herzl
   Amos Elon, *Herzl*, pp. 97-186, 221-47.
   Sachar, pp. 36-63.
   Hertzberg, pp. 204-30.
II. *Zionist Theory as Politics and Eschatology*
  Zionist Theory to 1948: Ahad HaAm. Klatzkin
   Sachar, pp. 65-138.
   Hertzberg, pp. 247-77, 314-28.
  Under the Mandate: Zionism and Socialism
   Sachar, pp. 138-62, 163-94, 249-78.
   Hertzberg, pp. 329-97.

CONTEXTS AND CURRICULA

      I LOVE YOU, ROSA, 7:30 p.m., Carmichael Auditorium
      Zionism and the Intellectuals
          Hertzberg, pp. 467–544.
III. *Zionism as Actuality: Israel and America*
      Zionism and the State of Israel
          Sachar, pp. 580–614, 667–740.
          Hertzberg, pp. 545–620.
          THE JAZZ SINGER, 7:30 p.m., List 120.
      Israeli Zionism Today
          Rael Jean Isaac, *Israel Divided*, pp. 1–73, 138–63.
          Sachar, pp. 740–838.
          Evening lecture on Israeli life today, David Goodblatt, Haifa University.
      NIGHT AND FOG. THE HOLOCAUST ("World at War"), 7:30 p.m., Carmichael Auditorium
      American Zionism and Palestinism ("Pro-Israelism")
          Yonathan Shapiro, *Leadership of the American Zionist Organization*, pp. 3–76, 207–61.
      The Zionist Critique of American Jewry
          Ben Halpern, *The American Jew*, pp. 11–69, 97–160.
      The Zionist Claim upon American Jewry
          Hillel Halkin, *Letters to an American-Jewish Friend*, pp. 1–76, 153–246.

VII. *A Personal Course: Judaism in Late Antiquity*

Finally I provide the syllabus of a course in which I introduce not a subject or a problem but something quite particular: my own work in its context. I think students should have access to the scholarly interests of professors, even though, in the nature of things, the larger work of teaching will require attention to larger and more representative aspects of a subject. Still, once in three or four years I give a course in which, in the main, the students read my work in the context of its larger historical and methodological setting: Judaism in late antiquity. The present version of the course required far too much reading and seemed to me to yield greater capacity to speak learnedly of problems of method than to form intelligent accounts of the character of the Judaism of ancient times and of the substance of its sources. I doubt that I would again offer the course in this particular formulation. But it may provide some idea of one approach to the problem of teaching one's own scholarly *oeuvres*, which I think does have a valid place within the undergraduate curriculum.

    The problem of this course is the description of Judaism out of the diverse sources—literary and archaeological—of the period 70 through 640.

Introduction to the Course
   I. *The World of Late Antiquity*
      The Tripartite World of Ancient Times: Iranian, Roman, and the Third World of Semitic and Other Peoples
      Peter Brown, *The World of Late Antiquity: From Marcus Aurelius to Muhammad*, pp. 7-188.
      M. Avi-Yonah, *The Jews of Palestine: A Political History from the Bar Kokhba War to the Arab Conquest.*
  II. *The Formation of Rabbinic Judaism: The Definition of Rabbinic Judaism*
      Neusner, *Between Time and Eternity*, pp. 1-114.
      _____, *Understanding Rabbinic Judaism*, pp. 1-336.
      The Formative Period of Rabbinic Judaism: Yavneh
      Neusner, *First-Century Judaism in Crisis: Yohanan ben Zakkai and the Renaissance of Torah*, pp. 1-200.
      _____, *Eliezer ben Hyrcanus*, vols. I-II.
      _____, *Development of a Legend: Studies on the Traditions concerning Yohanan ben Zakkai.*
      _____, *A Life of Yohanan ben Zakkai.*
 III. *Mishnah*
      Neusner, *Invitation to the Talmud: A Teaching Book*, pp. 1-87.
      _____, *A History of the Mishnaic Law of Purities*, II, pp. 221-56.
      _____, *The Rabbinic Traditions about the Pharisees*, Vol. III.
      _____, *Modern Study of the Mishnah.*
  IV. *Talmud*
      Neusner, *Invitation to the Talmud*, pp. 87-247.
      _____, *Formation of the Babylonian Talmud.*
   V. *Talmudic Judaism: The Use of Talmudic Evidence for the Study of Judaism*
      Neusner, *Talmudic Judaism in Sasanian Babylonia*, pp. 3-12.
      _____, *A History of the Jews in Babylonia*, III, pp. ix-xxi, 272-338; IV, pp. 183-278.
      _____, *A History of the Jews in Babylonia*, I (2nd ed.), pp. 122-78; II, pp. 92-125; III, pp. 41-271; IV, pp. 73-182.
      Cases, History, and History of Religions: The Rabbi
      Neusner, *Talmudic Judaism in Sasanian Babylonia*, pp. 25-138.
      _____, *A History of the Jews in Babylonia*, V, pp. 1-342.
  VI. *Synagogue Art: The Art of the Synagogue and the Religion of the Rabbis*
      Ernest Namenyi, *The Essence of Jewish Art*, pp. 1-80.
      Erwin Goodenough, *Jewish Symbols in the Greco-Roman Period*, XII, pp. 1-157.
      Pierre du Bourguet, *Early Christian Painting.*
      Neusner, *Early Rabbinic Judaism*, pp. 139-87.
      Smith, Review, *Journal of Biblical Literature* 86 (1967), pp. 53-68.
      Bernard Goldman, *The Sacred Portal: A Primary Symbol in Ancient Judaic Art.*
      Dura Europos and Its Synagogue
      Goodenough, *Jewish Symbols in the Greco-Roman Period*, XII, pp. 158-98.
      Carl Kraeling, *The Synagogue,* pp. 321-63.

        Neusner, *Early Rabbinic Judaism*, pp. 188-208.
        J. Gutmann, *The Dura-Europos Synagogue*.
        A. D. Nock, "The Synagogue Murals of Dura Europos," in *Harry A. Wolfson Jubilee Volume*, II.
        E. Bickerman, Review, in *Harvard Theological Review* 58 (1965), pp. 127-51.
        A. D. Nock, *Essays in Religion and the Ancient World*, ed. Zeph Stewart, I, pp. 459-68; II, pp. 877-918.
VII. *Archaeological Evidence of Judaism: The Magical Bowls*
        Neusner, *A History of the Jews in Babylonia*, V, pp. 217-44.
        _____, *Talmudic Judaism in Sasanian Babylonia*, pp. 13-24.
        M. Margaliot, ed., *Sefer Harazim*.
        M. Smith, "Hekhalot Rabbati," in A. Altmanr, ed., *Biblical and Other Studies*.
        Neusner, *History of the Jews in Babylonia*, V, pp. 343-75.
VIII. *Christian Writers on Judaism: Aphrahat*
        Neusner, *Aphrahat and Judaism*, pp. 1-18, 19-67, 63-83, 84-112, 113-22, 123-95, 196-241, 242-44.
        Robert Murray, *Symbols of Church and Kingdom*.
        A. Lukyn Williams, *Adversus Judaeos: A Bird's Eye View of Christian Apologiae until the Renaissance*.
        George F. Moore, "Christian Writers on Judaism," *Harvard Theological Review* 14 (1921), pp. 197-254.
IX. *Talmudic and Contemporary Judaism: The Uses of Talmudic Judaism by Modern Jews*
        Neusner, *Between Time and Eternity*, pp. 115-76.
        _____, *Contemporary Judaic Fellowship in Theory and in Practice*, pp. 1-50, 51-66, 67-74, 75-120, 121-48, 149-238, 239-70.

VIII. Conclusion

These syllabi are offered not principally to serve as models but primarily to stimulate others to give thought to the potentialities of the "introductory course." One kind of course which I do not offer is an introduction to Jewish religious belief and practice, to "the theology of Judaism," and to similar, essentially theological kinds of courses. The reason is that I think such courses obscure the critical problematic of studying Judaism as a contemporary religion. They impose upon the study of Judaism categories of greater value for the study of Christianity. The definition of what it is that we study when we study religion seems to me to require attention to religion not as theology and ritual but as an expression of a world-view and a way of living, as a mode of organizing society and creating and expressing culture. In these aspects the data for the Judaic experience are remarkably rich.

Moreover, within that definition supplied to us by anthropology, not theology, we are able to take seriously the "Jewishness" of people whose expression of Judaism diverges from the patterns conventionally understood as "religious"—no required believing, little churchgoing, for instance. These people experiment, in ways I think particularly interesting, with the potentialities of the Judaic tradition in the circumstances of modern and contemporary society. What is important about Judaism, so far as the Jews of modernity shape and express something legitimately deemed to fall within the tradition of Judaism, is not their irreligiosity (and I am not prepared to concede they are not "religious" in important suggestive ways). It is their capacity to revise and reshare inherited culture and tradition into something fully expressive of their humanity.

In short, Judaism must tell us how to introduce Judaism—Judaism, and not Christianity in its more conventional phases, or the model of any other important religion of our own day. Judaism will, for its part, make a contribution to the shaping of the definition of religion and of the agendum for the study of religion. But it can do so only when the interesting issues yielded by Judaism are permitted to stand at the head of the scholarly program. Telling our students "what the Jews believe" and how "the Jews practice their religion" describes only a part of the data, and, in my own judgment, not necessarily the most interesting part. Indeed, I should claim that the reason the study of Judaism finds so comfortable a niche in the humanities is the very complexity of the human data to be learned and interpreted.

CHAPTER 9
Contexts and Classrooms: Modes of Academic Advocacy. The Case of Judaism

When Jewish studies take place in synagogues and Jewish schools, they take up one set of quite legitimate and socially relevant tasks. When these same studies take place in a college or university, because of the utterly different setting, they take up a totally different set of quite legitimate and socially relevant tasks. What that means—and must mean—is that in no way are Jewish studies in universities continuous with Jewish studies in synagogue schools, high schools, yeshivot, youth programs, programs of study in the State of Israel, and the many other excellent modes in which Jewish learning is carried on under Jewish auspices and for Jewish purposes. Jewish studies in universities not only are not continuous with Jewish studies in parochial settings, but they are continuous with humanistic studies in universities. Students who pass from a course in philosophy or classics, history or literature, to a course in some aspect of Jewish learning do not move from the twentieth century to the tenth, and they also do not pass from neutral to holy territory. They are in the same university. They see the same faces. Professors talk with them in the same way, in the same language of thought and discourse, and, in a university worthy of the name, the range of issues of analysis and argument is essentially cogent and harmonious. That is what makes a university education distinctive.

When Jewish studies are pursued under parochial, Jewish auspices, whether they take place in a synagogue kindergarten or in a rabbinical seminary or yeshiva, their goal is to verify, validate, and vindicate the life and beliefs of the Jewish people. The paramount apologetic task of education is carried out in the right way, which is to say, not through apologetics but through technology which *assumes* the validity and veracity of that for which apology is required. Everyone knows what is commonly accepted. The propositions of the faith need no defense because they are spelled out within a closed system of society and mind. Since that is the case, the intellectual substance will be composed of three elements. First comes technology, as I said, the knowledge of how to read and write the given language of meaning. That is why stress is laid upon instruction in the Hebrew language, as though it were functional to American Jews. Second comes exegesis of texts. Here the apologetic is much clearer. "We all know" that the texts which are read are holy. "We all know" that there is reward in "learning" them. It follows that "we all know" that what is important is to say the words and explain the words. Why these texts and no others, why what is learned is self-evidently valid, and what these texts mean when put together with many other texts into a large and cogent picture of the whole—these are not useful questions, and they are not asked. The Jewish classroom, continuous with the Jewish pulpit, normally consists in the reading of a few lines of a text, followed by a few lines of commentary upon it, whether philological or homiletical. For it is only philology, on the one side, and homiletics, on the other, which serve. Third comes homiletics, divorced from exegesis of texts. Here the overwhelming power of the accepted ideology of Jewishness— that frame of "history-and-peoplehood" which is supposed to make sense of all and explain everything—is brought to bear. In this context scholarship is a tool of sanctification, and that which is to be sanctified is the student and the teacher, the congregation and the rabbi, the listener and the speaker.

This relationship of mutual validation and verification produces an agreed exchange. The people listen with awe and respect to the teacher, whether rabbi or professor or melamed. The teacher then praises the student and tells the listener what the student and listener are expected to hear: pretty much what they already know. The role of the teacher is not to surprise but to reassure, not to question but to answer questions, and above all, not to bring about the turning of the wheels of thought, but to make sure that, instead of turning, they merely spin.

It remains to observe that, for a people small in numbers and subject to intense pressures of disintegration, this system of education and mode of instruction are a natural remedy. The work of learning is indoctrination. In this instance, that which is to be indoctrinated is irrelevant to learning. It is loyalty, devotion, commitment, to something worthy of the same. And that is, to begin with, to the figure of authority—rabbi, teacher, melamed—who bestows, in exchange for loyalty, devotion, and commitment, a sense of self-worth and importance. It is a system of status conferred, and a world in which value is determined by consensus of sentiment. That is how a tradition preserves itself against change, and that is how, in its diverse settings, the Jewish group has determined to struggle for its life.

CONTEXTS AND CLASSROOMS

The reason that Jewish studies in university classrooms are discontinuous with Jewish studies in Jewish settings in particular is that universities are different from all other institutions of learning in our society in general. While they follow upon high school, in point of fact few university subjects are even taught in high school. I should guess that at least half of the departments of a liberal arts curriculum have no counterpart in the high school curriculum, or, at best, have so little place in the precollegiate program of studies as to be essentially absent, for instance, philosophy, economics, sociology, religious studies, engineering, and the like. Some subjects are carried through, for example, English, history, mathematics, foreign languages. But to that group are added many new ones, and, it goes without saying, there prevails a quite different attitude toward the whole.

Our task as teachers is different as well. In high schools the successful teacher wins the attention of his or her students to the subject at hand and teaches that subject. The work is to impart information, and success is measurable on college board exams. No one should underestimate the difficulties and challenge, since we have no natural constituency, in ordinary life, for the work of learning, beyond certain required skills of communication. Most of what children study in junior high school has no bearing upon the realities with which they cope; perhaps we thereby try to solve their problems by distraction. Most of what high school students study has no immediate application, and is not meant to, so that, just as before, it is no small work to win students' attention to the work and help them develop the will to learn. And the generality of high school teacher succeeds in that task.

In universities the successful teacher takes for granted the attention of the students because the students are present in a given course, while in most instances they are not required to be present. Consequently the work is not to interest the students. Nor is it solely to impart information, though that is an important part of the work. The center of the task is to begin the work of analysis, by which I mean, to help the student realize that knowledge is there to be taken apart and put back together, to be understood as system, process, or construction, and to make sense of the working of the system and the process, and the coherence of the construction. When the students' minds begin to move and to work, when important questions come to mind and can be distinguished from unimportant or irrelevant ones, when students learn how to listen to a lecture and intelligently to read and assess a book, and when they take on their task as participants in learning, then the work of the university has succeeded. Clearly, this work of analysis is meant to prepare students for important tasks, if not for specific jobs. University education insists that modes of critical thought and capacities for accurate perception and clear expression make a difference. They serve both to prepare for useful work and to make possible an interesting life. Learning is not "for its own sake," nor am I clear what "its own sake" consists of. Learning is for the accomplishment of certain concrete, socially relevant tasks. But these tasks are to be achieved in those particular ways in which universities have learned to do their work. If universities are not permitted to work in the ways they know, then they cannot be useful to the society or to the social class which sponsors them. Academic freedom is more than a slogan. It speaks to more than the situation of a holder of unpopular opinions (indeed, unfortunately, it seldom speaks to that one's situation at all). And the inner structures of peer review, faculty governance, collegiality, tenure, and those other dimly perceived and seldom understood institutions of university life hold up a widely perceived and generally understood world for learning. It all fits together. It all makes sense only when it fits together.

Enough has been said about these two utterly diverse, mutually unperceiving, worlds of Jewish schools and universities so that the obvious may now be stated very briefly. Jewish schools for Jewish learning and university programs in Jewish studies have nothing in common in their context, and therefore have nothing in common in anything but subject matter—if that. The theories of learning in these two distinct worlds are different, because the works of learning and its tasks are unrelated. I think the very theory of what learning is and how it works must be different, given the rather didactic and authoritarian character of the pulpit and its classroom equivalents in synagogues and yeshivot. Surely a system of learning garbed in theological splendor, in which one's very presence assures this-worldly esteem and other-worldly reward, cannot be compared to that other world in which learning is, at best, its own reward.

It must follow, in my view, that Jewish studies in university are simply not continuous with Jewish learning under Jewish auspices. The cognitive frames are distinct from one another, the social settings diverse, the constituencies utterly dissimilar, and the purpose of the one has no relationship to the purpose of the other. People have tended to argue that the difference between a professor in a theological seminary or yeshiva and one in a university is that the latter is not free to advocate, and the former is, or the former is not objective and the latter is. The categories are irrelevant to real life. We always advocate, and we never are objective: free of values. University professors of

Jewish studies care very deeply. Theologians who claim to teach something not laden with values are valueless to their students and to the world.

More important: the curriculum and methods of Jewish studies in university require formation in response to the particular educational tasks of the departmental setting and of the university's intellectual and social context. Precisely what response is to be recommended of course cannot be stated, since the contexts and purposes vary. In one setting emphasis may be upon the study of language and literature; in a second, upon the study of history, religion, culture, or philosophy; in a third, upon social traits and problems. What is forbidden is the essential replication of the curriculum of the Jewish schools, with their stress upon rote-learning of language and the technology of Jewish observance on the one side, and the apologetic of "history-and-peoplehood" on the other. The former is not relevant, the latter, not respectable, to this other context. When Jewish studies, in all their diversity and promise, find their place, in a university's taxonomy, under "exotic languages," then Jewish studies are effected in an impoverished way. When our principal concern is to impress our colleagues in the State of Israel or rabbis in pulpits with the continuity of our work with theirs, as is the case in many of the Hebrew programs and departments, then, again, Jewish studies are effected in a way which is awry. When nearly all the students in nearly all the courses are of Jewish origin, then Jewish studies have not yet found their way into the center of the humanistic or social scientific curriculum. The catalogue of deadly sins is not a long one, but the death is nonetheless as real. Nor is there a poison to the field more effective than to treat the Jewish studies professor as interchangeable with the local rabbi, or to have the rabbi serve to begin with as a professor, or to have the professor pretend to be a rabbi—or a Hillel director. None of this will do, and those who do not know why do not know the territory of universities. To be sure, they may know full well and not care.

Part III
Humanistic Approaches to the Study of Judaism
Theory and Practice

CHAPTER 10
Toward a Theory of Comparison: Alike and Not Alike. A Grid for Comparison and Differentiation

When we compare one thing to another, it is in order to gain a measure of perspective on each. What we seek is an account of likeness and difference, a mode of comparison, that is, finding the common ground; en route to differentiation, that is, discerning the uncommon too. Smith concludes his account of the problem with that point at which I wish to begin mine: "Wittgenstein's last question ['how am I to apply what the one thing shows me to the case of two things'] remains haunting. It reminds us that comparison is . . . never identity; it requires the postulation of difference as the grounds of it[s] being interesting (rather than tautological) and a methodical manipulation of difference, a playing across the 'gap', in the service of some useful end." Now there are two sides to the matter: comparison and differentiation. One without the other leaves us at that impasse at which Smith ends his reflections. But to escape therefrom we have to look beyond the barrier. We need to obtain a picture of the road beyond, that is, to define that useful end for which the work is done, the journey undertaken.

When we propose to differentiate, we postulate a fundamental commonality. When we propose to compare, we do so because we perceive some basic point of difference bearing significance. Comparison in a methodical way is a methodical manipulation of difference. Comparing and contrasting is to play across the gap. So let us begin with that "gap."

For historians of a religion, the gap is between not only different religions but one version of a religion and another one of the same religion. For historians of Judaism, the gap is not solely diachronic, that is, comparing the state of "Judaism" in Ezra's time, with that "Judaism" of the Essene community of Qumran, or with that "Judaism" of Maimonides. Indeed, the diachronic problem—how to construct or postulate a single "Judaism" spread out over so many centuries and countries, encompassing so vast a range of significant and definitive differences—is only part of the difficulty of description and definition in Judaism. The synchronic problem is no less acute. The varieties of ways of life and world-views exhibited by people who stoutly claim for themselves the title, "Israel," impress us in our own day. But it is hardly anachronistic to discern these same varieties in earlier times, whether we choose the second century B.C. and focus upon the diversity of Greek and Aramaic speaking Jews; or the second century A.D. and select Jews responsive to hopes for the end of days for comparison with those engaged in building an eternal system of sanctification; or address the third century and fourth century A.D. even in a single country, Babylonia, and notice there a quite severe conflict in theories of salvation with consequent difference in modes of attaining it; or speak of the ninth century with its Qaraites and Rabbinites; or the seventeenth with its Sabbateans and (from the Sabbatean viewpoint) infidels. This long catalogue is meant to underline a simple fact. The diversity of Judaisms generally characterizes not only the diachronic continuum, but also the synchronic frame, which sets bounds around the data deemed definitive of, and appropriate to, "Judaism."

It must follow that a sound definition of the labor of comparison and differentiation, a clear notion of what we do when we compare, and a defensible program of the exercises of description and interpretation these three tasks have to be successfully carried out if a religious tradition exhibiting any historical and cultural diversity is suitably to be grasped and subjected to analysis. Descriptive analysis of "a religion" is a labor of comparison and differentiation. To begin with, subject to the work of comparing and contrasting are the diverse systems of life and thought, the various societies or cultures, finding a place within said "religion." Because these systems or societies or cultures are alike, they can be shown to differ. Because there will be points of difference, one can discern commonalities and important traits of sameness. What the one thing shows me can be applied to two things *only* when both things show the same one thing (among other things).

The diachronic phenomena available for comparison in the history of Judaism pose one kind of problem, the synchronic phenomena, another.

In the case of Israelite systems of sanctification extending over that mythic "four thousand years" of current discourse, or, more concretely, at least three thousand, the problem is to establish grounds for comparison. Such a basis permits juxtaposing one world-view and way of life, constructed in the name of "Israel," with some other worldview and way of life, also constructed in the name of "Israel." The atomistic and nominalistic attack on a notion of a "Judaism" meant to deal with so vast a temporal range hardly requires amplification. When we ask what unites the historical David with David Ben Gurion, we come up with three answers, only the third of which is relevant in common discourse. The first is the theological answer, deriving, therefore, from the authoritative Talmudic stories about David as a master of Torah. So the diachronic unity gained through theology is imposed by theology; it need not detain us. Neither element of the comparison is taken seriously in its own context. The second is the psychological answer, deriving from the mind of David Ben Gurion, who (we may postulate, for the sake of argument) can have looked back upon a *soi-disant* ancestor for inspiration and example. While the psychological answer provides ample insight into the mind of an important twentieth century exemplar of "Israel," it provides nothing interesting for insight into the mind of an important tenth century B.C. framer of "Israel." So both parts of the comparison are not equal. The third is constituted by the claim that there indeed are points in common between King David and Prime Minister Ben Gurion. That claim proves less preposterous upon inspection than it does when it is laid down. For, after all, a common geographical location and a common set of military and political problems as points of commonality cannot be dismissed out of hand. That is what the one thing shows me which applies to the case of two things. But the diachronic comparison and contrast may rapidly collapse into a rubbish heap of platitudes, generalities, and commonplaces. The reason is that the fundamental justification for the exercise of comparison and contrast is not really well grounded to begin with. A running jump across the abyss of time and change between the one David and the other, as I said, cannot be confused with a leap of faith. Yet it is only a highly contemporary faith which justifies and validates the exercise of comparison.

That is why I think a more reliable route toward a theory of comparison and contrast is to be located in the diachronic setting, I mean, comparisons within a given age, defined by a common set of characteristics of a gross and obvious sort. These should be, to begin with, historical and geographic, cultural, political and economic and social. That is to say, within a given religious tradition extending over a long period of time and many countries, we must seek moments at which we may fairly and reliably speak of a particular place and time of proximate uniformity. Then, and only then, will the exercise of differentiation become possible, so that we may apply what the one thing shows me to the case of two things.

Finding what is unlike in the like is legitimate, in a way in which finding what is like in the unlike is not, because in the former case the datum is similarity, which is not imposed, imputed, or invented, but obvious and superficial. In the latter case the datum is difference, which also is not imposed, imputed, and invented. Then, if we wish to compare, our mental experiment is to differentiate among available similarities, rather than to wander aimlessly in search of connections. The latter process seems to me too much a labor of imagination or theology to serve well in the work of analysis and the gaining of insight.

So let us now specify those common grounds which make possible the mapping of diverse contours of a single social-religious group. If we are to compare artifacts of mind, then in common among the framers of those artifacts should be a common language and mode of discourse, even a shared holy book and doctrine about which to dispute. If we are to compare modes of constructing a holy way of life, we should locate a homogenous population, making its living within a single ecological and economic framework. Only in that way shall we be able to ascertain that points of difference do not express a merely economic or ecological diversity. If, finally, we propose to compare diverse visions of the meaning of history and the destiny of a group to which all parties claim to belong, we should begin the labor of comparison within the framework of a single political structure, or, at the least, a shared experience of politics. Otherwise those questions raised in peoples' minds about the meaning of history and the destiny of the group may turn out to be expressions of a diverse and incomparable political setting: different people ruled by different kings in different ways, so to speak. Finally, in common must also be sufficient data, so that we have not only ample knowledge of the several groups subject to comparison, but also knowledge of the same sort about these several groups. We cannot accomplish much, if for one group we know much about eschatology, and, for a second, about liturgical and cultic matters, and, for a third, about facts suitable for the comparison of the family and the writing of marriage contracts and writs of divorce. That rather obvious perquisite of comparative work has to be specified, because so much comparison has so far treated one thing about one group in juxtaposition to a totally incongruous thing about some other.

Now having listed what I think are the necessary outlines of a map for comparative studies, I may fairly be accused of traveling in search of an intellectual utopia. And yet, I think the conditions I have postulated can be met in more than a single moment in the history of Judaism(s) (to refer to the source of examples useful to the present exercise). Certainly the Jews of the Holy Land from the time of Ezra to the Moslem conquest can be shown to share a common language of mind and mode of discourse, Scripture. The economic and ecological framework remains fundamentally uniform, because of an unchanging natural habitat and enduring modes of production and exchange. All of the Jews of the country normally lived under a single government, even though, over time, the character and sponsorship of that government exhibited significant variation. Finally, a fair amount of data, both literary and material, have come under intensive study for a very long time. While we do not know all of the same things about a long series of diverse groups, all claiming to be "Israel," we do have access to some of the same things. The Gospels and the Mishnah come into contact at more than a few points, even though, on the surface, they are talking about different things to different people. So a labor of synchronic comparison, within a given period, will be worth attempting.

But the important question still remains to be asked, and it is phrased by Smith: "We know better how to evaluate comparisons, but we have gained little over our predecessors in either the method for making comparisons or the reasons for its practice. There is nothing easier than the discovery of similar patterns in a diversity of situations. . . . But the 'how' and the 'why' and, above all, the 'so what' remain most refractory. . . . It is a problem to be solved by theories and reasons, of which we have had too little." To phrase matters in another way: Having defined an arena for comparative study, why is it urgent to undertake this work of playing in the arena of comparison? What do we learn, which we did not know before, when we juxtapose two congruent (available) facts? What questions do we answer which we could not answer before the act of juxtaposition, comparison and contrast? Or, to put it more accurately: *What else do we know, what more do we know, than we knew before we tried to apply what the one thing shows me to the case of two things?* This is the significant issue.

My answer to this question comes out of a problem of interpretation thrown in my path by my own research, so with apology, I offer a minute of autobiography. In the course of studies leading to my *History of the Mishnaic Law of Purities* (Leiden, 1974–1977, vols. I–XXII), as in those culminating in the other components of the whole History of Mishnaic Law, I was struck by the problem of parallels. That is, I was well aware that in diverse cultures the corpse was a source of uncleanness, or that the transfer of a woman from man to man (e.g., father to husband) was carefully regulated, or that the advent of certain days in the lunar-solar cycle provoked in many social groups beside the Israelite one the application of taboos. I had to figure out what, if anything, I should do about those facts. I had to decide whether to assemble a range of parallel facts, and, if so, to choose those contexts suitable for a search for parallels, and to eliminate those unsuitable ones.

If composing a catalogue of cultures and circumstances in which a corpse produced "uncleanness" (or some other status not produced when the corpse is not present) would have materially assisted in my labor of describing and interpreting the Mishnaic law under discussion, I should have been ready (if not eager) to make up such a catalogue. It was at that point in my thinking that, I must admit, I began to raise questions about the value of comparison undefined by context and purpose. The "so what" of Smith's statement reinforced my instinct that the work was to no good end. This guess that the labor would be futile provoked a search for how to make the work worthwhile. I could not ignore the obvious fact that corpses do "contaminate" nearly everywhere. I also could not make sense of how to utilize that fact, e.g., for the interpretation of the same fact in the setting of Mishnaic law. That is to say, What else do I know, what more do I know, than I knew before I discovered that one thing, the fact of corpse-"contamination" is the case of two things (indeed, of many things).

Two steps forward marked my progress. The first came with the work on *Purities*, the second, on *Women*. In the former, I noted that a fact has to be interpreted within its own context, and, once in that context, becomes particular to it. In this regard I found particularly suggestive the statement of Mary Boyce on the simple fact that eschatological doctrines of Zoroaster occur in four great religions, Judaism, Christianity, Islam, as well as in Zoroaster's own religion. She states:

> Zoroaster's eschatological teachings . . . became profoundly familiar through borrowings, to Jews, Christians, and Muslims, and have exerted enormous influence on the lives and thoughts of men in many lands. Yet it was in the framework of his own faith that they attained their fullest logical coherence. . . .

In that context, this judgment of Boyce's means that comparison yields little insight beyond the simple fact that the same thing is found in more than one place. My own comment at that point was this: "While a woman after childbirth is deemed unclean for the same forty days in both the Zoroastrian and the Israelite Levitical systems of uncleanness, the meaning of that shared detail is different for each context, and knowledge of the fact on its own produces no insight." The presence of one rule in two different cultures could not be interpreted or explained. For whatever significance that shared fact had was particular to the cultures in which it made its appearance. Differing verbal explanations were all that I had in hand, unless I wished to follow the example of Goodenough in positing some meaning of a universal and a psychological

TOWARD A THEORY OF COMPARISON

character present in the underground of a given fact. That example did not seem to me promising or fructifying. It follows that had matters stood as they then appeared, the entire exercise of comparison should have proved futile. Even if we found logical ground for uncovering similar patterns in a diversity of situations, we could not then say, "So what? Because...."

The second step, in the context of my *History of the Mishnaic Law of Women*, was to recognize that, if a fact appearing in many systems became consequential only in the context of those several systems, then comparison may be attempted among systems joined by said common fact. Specifically, what was to be compared was the principle of selection which led a given society to choose for its sustained attention one fact, rather than some other. Why a given system talks about the documentation of the transfer of women while another speaks about the prohibitions of consanguinity, the behavior of mothers in relationship to children, or the sexual activities of women at diverse points in their relationship to men—these are questions which may lead to comparison of system to system. Answers to these kinds of questions about principles of selection and their practical exegesis and application permit us to compare and contrast the *choices* made by diverse groups. We thereby may hope to understand the taxonomy of systems, both within a given cultural framework and even across frontiers of space and time. The work of systemic description is to compare one system with some other, to uncover principles of selection and the logic operative within each, and the relationships of those principles and that logic to the encompassing ecological framework (using the word ecology in a social and historical sense) among the several systems under study. Our work then is to locate the logic of a given system and to relate that logic to the context of the system. Meaning is to be perceived in two dimensions, first, within the system located and constructed in context, second, between diverse systems yielded by a shared context. Context then is not *a priori*, but merely prior to the work of interpretation. So the work, as it seemed in connection with *Women*, was to find out what makes a system systematic.

At this point I must digress to emphasize that when we speak of system, we mean only a social system. That is a way of seeing the world and living life characteristic of a specific, bounded group of people, way of life and world-view which work together to define the group and make sense of its collective life, keeping the outsider outside and joining the insiders together into the group. The boundaries of a system are the boundaries of the group, the things which make the group distinctive among systemic constructions. These are the encompassing mode of living, the comprehensive mode of explanation. The limits of the system are not literary but social, even though, in historical research, we tend to begin with literary evidence. But we end with a material description of a system of social group, a description so composed as to permit the juxtaposition and comparison of one system created by one social group with another system expressive of the totality of being of some other.

Having offered an answer to the question of *how*, I turn now to the twin questions: *Why? So what?* Once more I find it best to offer an answer out of my own autobiography. Why do I wish to construct a system out of law and to make sense of the whole by seeking other wholes, other systems? The answer is given in the question, in the use of the language, "to make sense." In my judgment knowing what a given group has to say about its life by itself does not help us to make sense of what that group wishes to say. It is only in discovering the choices, the contexts in which statements are made, in defining the persistent questions to which statements constitute answers, that the statements begin to make sense. Discovering similar patterns in a diversity of situations makes possible the juxtaposition for purposes of contrast and of comparison of the people who live in those circumstances and make their lives within them.

Only when we take account of the things people might have done are we able to make sense of the things they actually did do. Confronting the range of choices, we make sense of the chosen. Now since a given group generally does some one thing, constructing the requisite group of choices is rarely possible within the range of artifacts of a single group. I suppose in theory all the things all groups might choose constitute the true range of alternatives, a social and cultural equivalent to the unlimited range of sounds we are able at birth to replicate. But in practice, a broader synchronic context, defined as I did earlier in terms of commonalities of politics, economics, and culture, defines the proximate range of alternatives, equivalent to the sounds we actually hear, which rapidly deprive us of our innate power to make all sounds ever heard. I apply what the one thing shows me to the case of two things by demonstrating that, faced with both things, one group chose one thing, one group the other. In the comparison and contrast of groups standing within a single, clearly defined continuum, I am able to make sense of one group by playing it off against the other. The useful end of the game of comparison, then, is to show, through the might-have-beens of culture, to discover the meaning of what was.

The chief perplexity, the purpose of contrast and comparison, and the end of insight, is to show the relationship between peoples' ways of viewing the world and living out life, on the one side, and the context in which sight becomes insight, and a way of life, the stuff of living. These then are the decisive questions: What questions are answered, and how are they answered, in the system of historical and social ecology framed and founded by a given group? How do others answer these same questions, within the same systematic structure of history and economy? And, finally, what do we learn about both groups in the comparison and contrast of each to the other? These are the three exercises which respond to the questions, "Why?" "So what?" For the answer to "so what" must be, So this is one way in which people made choices, and that is another way, and in the variables between the one and the other lie rich insight even into how we are and might be.

What I propose, therefore, is a way beyond the historicizing atomism which treats all things as unconnected to all others, and which therefore closes off the path to insight worth sharing, method worth repeating. Historians treat events as singular. That is why events deserve careful description. But if there are patterns, they reduce the singularity, the givenness, of the singular. To historians the search for insight is for philosophers, theologians, or social scientists—people who wish to bring things into relationship and find out the universally useful truth in diverse things. Now the power of historical study also is its pathos, just as the strength of philosophy and theology is their weakness. To take the case at hand, the theological construction of *Judaism* falls before the swinging pendulum of historians, with their exceptions, their various examples, their particulars. And yet in the detritus of history still are bricks and stones. The iron ball does not smash all. Out of the ruins will emerge new buildings, made of the bricks of the old, the irreducibles of society, the not-to-be-pulverized facts of ongoing material life and shared, enduring imagination alike.

So there is no possibility of claiming there never was, nor is there now, such a thing as "Judaism," but only "Judaisms." For once we take that route, there will be no "Judaisms" either, but only this one and that one, and how we feel from day to day, and this morning's immutable truth and tradition. But to find that alternative way historians of religions need not magically turn themselves into philosophers or theologians. Their work of patient description of some one thing, one at a time, which is their power, cumulatively yields descriptions of diverse things, all together, all at once. Seeing the whole whole, finding out what makes it whole, establishing definitive context, discovering the questions to which systems constitute answers—this is the sort of description which makes possible the labor of interpretation. And that work of interpretation begins when the work of description has made available two or more sets of interesting facts, I mean, when the work of description has shown that the one thing applies to the case of two things. Out of description then comes that work of interpretation, which, in my judgment, is an exercise of comparison, and therefore contrast: a labor of nuanced comparison and differentiation. To sum up: the ideal things to compare with one another are snowflakes—or religions.

CHAPTER 11
Toward a Theory of Category-Formation: Shaping Useful Categories. The Problem of "Judaism," "Christianity," and "Hellenism"

When we speak of "Judaism," "Christianity," or "Hellenism,"[1] for the period under discussion, we use terms of our own making, to collect and contain data of our own choosing. These terms permit us to systematize, interpret, and compare entities which, essentially, we ourselves have created. For, as everyone knows, the category of "Judaism" in antiquity did not mean what it now does, and just as Israelites did not call their religion-culture "Judaism," so Christians did not call theirs, "Christianity," but "the Way." By "Hellenism" people meant (and mean) little or much, for a Hellene could be a person who speaks Greek, and it could be someone whose values and way of living were conveyed by the adjective, and it could be many sorts of people in between those two extremes.[2] Since, as we all know, for about a century Christians regarded themselves as part of Israel, it surely is difficult to utilize the stated category. I need hardly rehearse in the present circumstance the old familiar fact that there was no "normative Judaism," that the use of the term "orthodox" for any of the sorts of Judaism about which the first century informs us is simply witless anachronism, and that, it must follow, the sole "Judaism" deserving the term "normative" or, at least, descriptively "normal," is the kind for which we have scarcely any documentation, I mean, the religion of the vast majority of the ordinary Israelites in the Holy Land, those who are not represented by any of the surviving sectarian literature.

---

[1] This note carries forward my discussion, "'Judaism' after Moore," *Journal of Jewish Studies* 1980, 2. It is my contribution to the symposium, "Early Christianity at the Crossroads of Judaism and Hellenism," Society of Biblical Literature Annual Meeting, Dallas, Texas, November 6, 1980, chaired by Professor Helmut Koester, Harvard University, with Adela Yarbro Collins, McCormick Theological Seminary, and Harold Attridge, Southern Methodist University.

[2] Surely the polemical usage in the Maccabean context cannot be permitted to exhaust the possibilities.

While, to be sure, the "Judaism" of the Israelites of the Holy Land may well stand description upon the basis of the sources we do have, I cannot think of a single book on that subject. The highly suggestive and I think absolutely sound description of my teacher, Morton Smith, in *Jesus the Magician*, in this context deserves more than the very brief citation which I can supply, as follows:

> The picture of the world common to Jesus and his Jewish Palestinian contemporaries is known to us from many surviving Jewish and Christian documents. It was wholly mythological. Above the earth were heavens inhabited by demons, angels, and gods of various sorts (the "many gods") whose existence Paul conceded in I Cor. 8.5, and among whom he counted "the god of this age," II Cor. 4.4). In the highest heaven was enthroned the supreme god, Yahweh, "God" *par excellence*, who long ago created the whole structure and was about to remodel, or destroy and replace it. Beneath the earth was an underworld, to which most of the dead descended. There, too, were demons. Through underworld, earth, and heavens was a constant coming and going of supernatural beings who interfered in many ways with human affairs. Sickness, especially insanity, plagues, famines, earthquakes, wars, and disasters of all sorts were commonly thought to be the work of demons. With these demons, as with evil men, particularly foreign oppressors, the peasants of Palestine lived in perpetual hostility and sporadic conflict, but the relations were complex. As the Roman government had its Jewish agents, some of whom, notably the Herods, were local rulers, so the demons had their human agents who could do miracles so as to deceive many. The lower gods were the rulers of this age, and men who knew how to call on them could get their help for all sorts of purposes. So could women, whose favors they had rewarded by teaching them magic and other arts of civilized life. On the other hand, Yahweh, like the demons, was often the cause of disasters, sickness, etc., sent as punishments. He sometimes used angels, sometimes demons, as agents of his anger, and his human agents, his prophets, could also harm as well as help. Most Jews believed that in the end he would destroy or remodel the present world, and create a new order in which the Jews, or at least those who had followed his law, would have a better life. However, as to the course of events and the actors in the coming catastrophe, there was wide disagreement; any number of contradictory programs circulated, with various roles for one or more "messiahs"—special representatives of Yahweh—anti-messiahs, and assorted mythological monsters.[3]

Smith concludes this passage, "This was the picture of the world common in first century Palestine." Hence, if we wish to describe the world-view and the way of life of Judaism of the period in which Christianity was taking shape, this is the "Judaism" at the point at which "Christianity" approached that crossroads. But, then, "Christianity" is part of this kind of Judaism.

---

[3] Morton Smith, *Jesus the Magician* (N.Y.: 1978), pp. 4–5. For a picture of how I believe one should deal with evidence pertinent to a more limited group than "Israel" as a whole, see my *Judaism: The Evidence of the Mishnah* (Chicago: 1981).

A THEORY OF CATEGORY

When we come to "Hellenism," our problem of definition is much more complicated, since "Hellenism" is not a cultural category distinctive to the Holy Land. But so far as people have used "Hellenism" as an organizing and differentiating category, they have tended to deem "Hellenism" to be distinct from "Judaism." In fact, we must note, "Christianity" and "Judaism" are part of this same "Hellenism." For in light of Smith's comments just now cited, the issue of how different the world-view of "normative Judaism" and the world-view of an equivalently widely-diffused "Hellenism" were from one another remains to be confronted. But it is hardly a confrontation demanding our immediate engagement. For, in fact, to see "Judaism" and "Hellenism" as essentially separate and distinct worlds is to see the world as it was seen for a mere century before the scholarly achievements of the middle of the twentieth century, and it is *not* to see it as we now do.

The simple fact is that the Holy Land had been thoroughly and completely Hellenized long before the advent of Christianity. In this regard, in his *Palestinian Parties and Politics that Shaped the Old Testament*,[4] Morton Smith states what I believe to be the presently regnant, and right, consensus, when he writes, "The four hundred and twenty years between Nebuchadnezzar's destruction of Jerusalem (587) and the outbreak of the Maccabean revolt (167) saw an immense cultural change. . . . This change is usually described as 'Hellenization.' The term is unfortunate, since it suggests that the change was due entirely to imitation of Greek ways. That was not the case, but much of the change was due to Greek influence, and the dominant elements in some aspects of the resultant culture—notably in language, in design and decoration, in business, in scholarship, and in technology—were Greek." The process encapsulated by the word "Hellenization" would be better characterized, in context, as an experience which, today, we should call, for lack of better language, "modernization," or, in the setting of the third world, "Westernization." The changes were much the same.

The discussion by Smith, in a book originally completed in 1957, brought together in one place a vast amount of data and totally made sense of those data. Along these same lines, Saul Lieberman's *Greek in Jewish Palestine* and *Hellenism in Jewish Palestine*, now in print for better than thirty years, had long since demonstrated that Greek modes of thought and philosophical and rhetorical expression had penetrated even into those documents universally deemed to be particularly and quintessentially "Judaic," namely, the two Talmuds and cognate writings of the later rabbis.

[4] *Palestinian Parties and Politics that Shaped the Old Testament* (N.Y.: 1971), p. 57.

When we come to consider the category, "Hellenism," therefore, we have to take account of the present state of learning, which Smith summarizes as follows:

> When all these factors are considered—repeated military conquest, constant military occupation, Greek settlement both in cities and in the countryside, economic and administrative penetration which reached every village, systematic exploitation of the countryside through landed estates, Palestinians' dealings with Phoenicians and Egyptians, and Jewish ties with Jews of the diaspora—when all these factors are considered it is clear that the cultural history of Palestine from the beginning of the Persian period is one of constant subjection to Greek influence, and that already in the Ptolemaic period every sector of the country must have been shaped by that influence more or less. "More or less" implies differences of degree which were undoubtedly important, but there were only differences of degree. As the evidence has shown, some of the most important elements of Greek culture had everywhere come to be taken for granted: typically Greek artifacts and techniques were everywhere in use; the country had a monetary economy, foreign trade was a major concern, the frame of thought had ceased to be the land of Palestine and become the civilized world, and Greek had become—as it was throughout that world—the normal language of business and politics.[5]

It should be clear, finally, that Martin Hengel's *Judaism and Hellenism*[6] stands at the center of contemporary learning and does the necessary labor of stating matters as they should be seen. In the summary of Louis H. Feldman,[7] Hengel argues two basic theses: "(1) we must cease to differentiate the Judaism of the land of Israel from Hellenistic Judaism, since both show deep Greek influence; and (2) this influence was pervasive at a much earlier point than had been previously thought, in fact at least a century before the Maccabean revolt in 168 B.C.E." Feldman's scholastic exercise—a kind of *sic et non*, in which Hengel provides the *sic*, and Feldman, the *non*—need not detain us. The twenty-two proofs Feldman attributes to Hengel, and Feldman's own twenty-two disproofs, really do not get us close to the center of Hengel's thesis, which pertains to society and culture, let alone to the simple truths Smith had brought together long before, in his 1957 dissertation.

---

[5] *Palestinian Parties*, pp. 72–73.

[6] Martin Hengel, *Judaism and Hellenism. Studies in their Encounter in Palestine during the Early Hellenistic Period* (Philadelphia: 1974) I–II. Translated by John Bowden from the German: *Judentum und Hellenismus* (1969).

[7] Louis H. Feldman, "Hengel's *Judaism and Hellenism* in Retrospect," *Journal of Biblical Literature* 96, 3, 1977, pp. 371–82. Cited: p. 371. Feldman's mode of toting up the "proofs" and systematically "refuting" them is puerile, and the critique of Hengel immaterial to the main thesis.

A THEORY OF CATEGORY

I think Hengel's basic view of the matter is correct. But the debate cannot be phrased in terms of the true meaning of "Hellenism" or "Judaism"—surely not alone in the setting of the Maccabean wars. That will not get us very far, as Feldman's attempted "refutation" of Hengel proves. Hengel is completely right in insisting that we not differentiate religious from political forces (p. 307), and the categories of "paganism," and "syncretism," for that matter, will have to be reconsidered with some care and endowed with nuance. For his part, I think Hengel's resort to the simplistic category, "Judaism," will have to give way. In fact, we must begin to differentiate, not between the Judaism of the Land of Israel and Hellenistic Judaism, but among diverse sorts of Judaism, so far as we have information about them, within a single but diverse and nuanced matrix of Hellenistic politics, economy, and culture: a modern world of antiquity. Only in that way shall our categories begin to serve us to organize and differentiate the data in our hand.

What is wrong is the (premature) use of these -isms and -ities. That is to say, we systematize too soon. We attempt to pour into our systematic categories too many facts, data deriving from too broad a range of communities and contexts. We too rapidly categorize through homogenization what in fact should be allowed to stand differentiated, to await interpretation in terms of particular to the segment of the data in hand. What must be proved, first of all, is that we do deal with an organizing category, with things which fall together and so permit us to interpret a particular corpus of data as a single cultural phenomenon, a cogent social system. Once we have shown that, in hand, we have data which stand description within a single frame of interpretation, that is, once we do have a social group with a distinctive and distinguishing world-view and way of life, then, with some reservations, we may begin to speak of the doctrine and way of life of that group as an -ism or an -ity. But the groups of which we shall speak, while more than a mass of isolated individuals(!), will be much less than that "Judaism" or that "Hellenism" or that "Christianity" which, too soon and for the wrong reasons, we nowadays attempt to place into relationship, and to compare, with one another.

CHAPTER 12
Toward a Theory of Talmudic "Lives": The Present State of Rabbinic Biography

Let us begin with the question of what we know about the ancient rabbis, those named in Mishnah and related literature, in current scholarship.[1] A considerable scholarly program, that devised by me, now has been achieved, and we are able to see firm results accomplished in that program. I refer, specifically, to the study of the lives and thought of the rabbis—"tannaim"—who are supposed to have flourished between the destruction of the Second Temple in A.D. 70 and the advent of Bar Kokhba in A.D. 132, and who are therefore associated with the period, if not the locus, of Yavneh. From my *Life of Yohanan ben Zakkai*,[2] which marks the end of an old epoch in methodology, a series of studies and dissertations has been successfully accomplished.[3] These have repeatedly produced these significant results.

---

[1] By *current* I mean the period since 1960. During that time I know of not a single book in Hebrew or any Western language on the life and teaching of a particular rabbinical authority of the first and second centuries (excluding Y. D. Gilat's *Eliezer ben Hyrcanus*, which I shall soon publish in English in *Studies in Judaism in Late Antiquity* [E. J. Brill]), which is not written by myself or one of my students or former students. Work coming out of the State of Israel is not, in the main, concerned with history or the history of ideas and of religions at all. Such history as has come forth in that period—mainly short articles on this and that—has been notorious for its primitive use of evidence and its slovenliness, since the scholars do not seem even to think necessary the analysis of all available evidence in all its diverse versions. They are satisfied to cite a few stories or sayings, without analysis of any serious kind—whether literary or conceptual or even philological—as ample evidence of the state of mind of a particular authority. While these deplorable traits characterize such work as has come from the Western scholars, as exemplified by Judah Goldin's paper on 'Aqiba in *Journal of the American Oriental Society*, Vol. 96, 1976, pp. 38–56, attention to the Israeli work in this same area will show still more disheartening tendencies. It therefore is not yet possible to cite important books and major research projects undertaken outside of the circle whose work is reported here.

[2] *A Life of Yohanan ben Zakkai, Ca. 1–80 C.E.* Second edition, completely revised. (Leiden: 1970).

[3] These studies and dissertations are as follows: J. Neusner, *Eliezer ben Hyrcanus. The Tradition and the Man* (Leiden: 1973), I–II; Gary Porton, *The Traditions of Rabbi Ishmael* (Leiden: 1976–), I–IV; William Scott Green, *Joshua ben Hananian* (Leiden: 1981), I–III; Shamai Kanter, *Gamaliel of Yavneh* (Chico: 1980), I; Charles Primus, *'Aqiba's Contribution to the Law of Zera'im* (Leiden: 1977); Jack N. Lightstone, *Yose the Galilean* (Leiden:

First, in the study of the traditions attributed to, and stories told about, earlier rabbis, we have to take account of three wholly distinct types of material, which seem to have no influence upon or connection with, one another. These are legal, exegetical, and "biographical." The legal materials attributed to all of the rabbis of Yavneh occur beginning in the earliest rabbinic document, Mishnah-Tosefta, and in general unfold, where the history can be assessed, in a disciplined and orderly way. As I show in *Eliezer*, what is attributed to Eliezer b. Hyrcanus by his immediate disciples and contemporaries will unfold in later strata, in a consistent way both literary and attributive, and will never then be contradicted. Moreover, pericopae bearing evidence of later origination, e.g., in documents after Mishnah, or bearing attestations of authorities of the third and fourth centuries, fall nearly wholly within the thematic framework established by materials bearing earlier attestations or occurring in Mishnah. This means that, in the area of legal sayings, there was no tendency promiscuously and without clear warrant to attribute to Eliezer whatever people wanted. On the contrary, there seems to have been a rather disciplined effort to amplify and augment materials assigned to him solely within the conception and principles already established in his name. This is a sign that the unfolding of the legal tradition in the three or four hundred years after the turn of the second century was governed by attention to what is said in the name of the earlier authorities and will not be characterized by attribution to an early authority of an idea first invented later on, for instance for the purpose of securing for that new idea the prestige of the name of the revered and ancient master.

When, by contrast, we come to exegetical materials, that is, sayings on the meaning of Scriptural verses given in the name of Yavnean authorities, we find it simply impossible to relate what is said on Scripture to what is said on law. Time and again, the students of the traditions assigned to Yavnean rabbis have been stymied by the problem of how to relate the exegetical to the legal corpus. What they find in Genesis Rabbah or Leviticus Rabbah, the earliest compilations of exegetical sayings, and what they find in Mishnah and in Tosefta, or

---

1978), I; Tzvee Zahavy, *The Traditions of Eleazar ben Azariah* (Missoula: Brown Judaic Studies, Scholars Press, 1977); Joel Gereboff, *Tarfon* (Missoula: Brown Judaic Studies, Scholars Press, 1978). In addition, shorter studies on traditions attributed to the men of the Great Assembly, Sadoq, Eleazar Hisma, and some other minor figures are analyzed by several authors in William Scott Green, ed., *Persons and Institutions in Earlier Rabbinic Judaism* (Missoula: Brown Judaic Studies, Scholars Press, 1977). My *Rabbinic Traditions about the Pharisees before 70* (Leiden: 1971), I–III, treats all figures assumed to have been Pharisees in the period before the destruction.

even in the two Talmuds, are simply without perceived relevance to one another. Nor are the exegetical materials themselves susceptible to the sort of study of development and disciplinary amplification referred to in connection with the legal ones. In the exegetical compilations, Eliezer, Ishmael, Tarfon, and Gamaliel simply supply names, to which exegeses are assigned without (as-yet-perceived) rhyme or reason. The exception will have reference in the legal exegetical compilations, particularly Sifra and Sifré, to legal rulings of Mishnah-Tosefta, in which case the point is to demonstrate that said rulings derive from exegesis, not from reason. These self-evidently are secondary to, and dependent upon, Mishnah-Tosefta and in no way change the picture.[4]

As to "biographical" materials, by which are meant moral sayings or non-legal stories in which a rabbi's name is mentioned, these are of two kinds. In the first, a rabbi's name is used without any clear claim that a particular individual and his intellectual or moral straits come under discussion. There will be set sequences of names, e.g., Eliezer, Joshua, Gamaliel, 'Aqiba, but what is said about, or done with, those names bears no relationship whatever to biography, that is, to what a particular individual said or did. In the second, a particular rabbi's name is used in a clearly homiletical story, e.g., how Tarfon tended to his mother's needs. Even if we were to believe all of the stories presented as "biographical," we should have very little biography for the earlier rabbis. The reason is that the homilies all together add up to no effort, even casual and unsystematic, to record what a given authority really said or did through a significant part of his lifetime. The blatant homiletical purpose precludes biography in these "biographical" materials.

It follows that the three kinds of materials given in the name of a particular rabbi bear virtually no internal interrelationships, on the one hand, and clearly must be used for purposes other than the composition of biographies, on the other. For even if we concentrate on the legal sayings, inclusive of the stories of various types, whether precedents or illustrations, we come to insuperable problems. These are generated by the documents in which said sayings occur. If we were to propose to describe a given authority's legal ideas, that is, his religious philosophy expressed through concrete teachings on the conduct of ordinary life, we should want to begin with some evidence that what a given authority is supposed to have said really has been said by him. Otherwise, our account of his legal ideas really is not intellectual

---

[4] Compare my *History of the Mishnaic Law of Purities*. VII. *Negaim. Sifra* (Leiden: 1975), pp. 1–12, 211–30.

biography at all. But when we approach the diverse documents of the law, we find that the sayings attributed to all authorities are given in highly patterned and stereotype language, so that it is hardly possible to claim that, to begin with, we have in our hands anything like *ipsissima verba*. We may very well have access to what an authority thought. But we rarely can demonstrate that what he thought has been preserved in the works in which he expressed his thought, and we often can demonstrate the opposite. For Mishnah-Tosefta is a document formulated in the processes of redaction, and what the redactors have done to create Mishnah, in particular, is to revise the whole of the received corpus into the language and redactional constructions of their own preference.[5] I am inclined to think that, prior to the time of Our Holy Rabbi, materials were collected along the lines of a single authority's name, of a single formal pattern, or of a single principle of law affecting diverse topics of law. But Rabbi's preference clearly is to group materials not in the name of a given authority, form, or abstract principle, but, essentially, topically, even though the sherds and remnants of materials brought together along other lines do remain in our hands. It follows, in any event, that while what is attributed to a given authority may or may not derive from him or his circle of disciples, we have no hope of presenting sizable bodies of sayings in the exact words spoken by a given authority.

Since these are the facts, it must be concluded that the effort to recover the biographies of individual rabbis of the late first and early second centuries is not feasible. Whether or not the same conclusion pertains to the rabbis who lived in the later second century seems to me not in doubt, since the literary facts pertinent to ʿAqiba apply without much variation to Judah, Simeon, Meir, or Yosé. But the state of the question for the rabbis of the third and fourth centuries is apt to be shaped by the nature of the quite different processes of literary formulation and transmission which produced the Talmuds in which their materials in the main are preserved, on the one side, and those same processes which yield the Midrashic compilations, on the other. These have not been critically assessed in detail, so we cannot yet come to conclusions on the promise of rabbinic biography for the Amoraic period.

We hardly are justified, however, to conclude that we learn nothing about earlier Rabbinic Judaism from the study of the sayings and stories assigned to its founding generations. On the contrary, once we

---

[5] This is demonstrated at some length and systematically in my *History of the Mishnaic Law of Purities, XXI. The Redaction and Formulation of the Order of Purities in Mishnah and Tosefta* (Leiden: 1977). I must say I find these results disturbing.

A THEORY OF TALMUDIC "LIVES"

ask the correct questions, we find we learn much worth knowing. In the study of the history and character of the traditions in the names of Yavneans, for example, we learn what it was important to say about those authorities in the times in which those responsible for the later compilations did their work. We notice, first of all, that in the third and fourth and later centuries, the telling of stories about earlier rabbis was deemed an important part of the work of traditioning and handing on the Tannaitic corpus. Men who, in their own day and for a century thereafter, are important, e.g., in Mishnah-Tosefta, principally in connection with opinions in their names on mooted legal topics of Mishnah-Tosefta, now, in the strata of the Talmuds and in the other Midrashic compilations require yet another treatment entirely. They must be turned into paragons of virtue and exemplars of the values of the growing rabbinic movement. Long after their legal traditions had come to closure, their biographies continue to grow, in response to a self-evident need to expand the modes by which Rabbinic tradition would express itself and preserve and impart its teachings. The histories of the traditions of the several authorities of Yavneh[6] prove beyond doubt that it is in the third and fourth centuries—the age of Roman prosopographia—that the telling of stories about rabbis of the first and second centuries, the making up of homilies about their deeds, and the provision of a more human visage for the ancient authorities, became urgent in the Rabbinic circles of both Palestine and Babylonia.

It furthermore should not be supposed that the attribution of sayings to authorities of the late first and second centuries bears no consequences for the study of the history of earlier Rabbinic Judaism. The contrary is the case. For we are able to devise a method by which

---

[6] These histories have not been entirely worked out yet, since, as is clear (above, note 1), the analysis of the traditions is still in process. My *Development of a Legend. Studies on the Traditions concerning Yohanan ben Zakkai* (Leiden: 1971), pp. 265–301, indicates the sort of work to be done. That early work also explores a number of other kinds of problems entirely, e.g., the issue of how to deal with diverse versions of what appears to be a single story; how to contend with the versions of a single saying in several successive documents and how to construct the necessary tables and charts to come to grips with the state of the entirety of a given rabbi's tradition. Had that book, in its day, been given the advantage of intelligent reviews by others, rather only than the extended critique by myself and my own circle (compare *Eliezer ben Hyrcanus*, II, pp. 437–58), it would have saved others the need to repeat the processes and to replicate the exact results achieved by me. After that book appeared, at least two extended comparisons of the Merkabah-stories told about Yohanan ben Zakkai in Tosefta, Babli, and so on, were printed, one in English, the other in French. Neither of these in *any* way revised the results produced by me in the comparison of the several versions and in the meaning of the results thereof. Neither "scholar" evidently had done his homework and so both were condemned to needless labor.

we may test part of what is alleged in those attributions, which is that said sayings belongs at a given point in the history of Rabbinic legal thinking, and not later. If to 'Aqiba is assigned a saying which in conception and logic is prior to one attributed to Judah or Meir, of the next generation, and which furthermore appears to generate the conception attributed to Judah or Meir, then we may fairly conclude that to the time of 'Aqiba belongs the conception of the saying given in his name. That sort of conclusion may not appear so satisfying, but upon that basis a fairly firm and solid history of the law and its religious and philosophical conceptions is to be worked out. That kind of history[7] in no way depends upon whether or not 'Aqiba really said what is attributed to him, but only upon whether we are able to find evidence that what is assigned to 'Aqiba or any other Yavnean is prior in conception or principle to what is assigned to Judah or Meir or any other Ushan, after Bar Kokhba. Upon that basis a history of the unfolding of the law is to be founded, and the sort of history of ideas further may be correlated with the great events of the age to which, it would seem reasonable, the rabbis' thinking upon any important question must have responded. Once the history of the law is worked out for Mishnah-Tosefta, we should have a fair picture of the foundations of the earlier stages of Rabbinic Judaism. These in turn will delineate the work which must follow.

[7] It is exemplified in my *History of the Mishnaic Law of Purities* (Leiden: 1974–1977), I-XXII; *History of the Mishnaic Law of Holy Things* (Leiden: 1979–), I-VI; and my students' *History of the Mishnaic Law of Agriculture*, of which the first part, Richard S. Sarason, *Demai* (Leiden: 1979) is now in print. The other tractates are presently underway, as follows: *Berakhot*, Tzvee Zahavy; *Peah*, Charles Primus; *Kilaim*, Irving Mandelbaum; *Terumot*, Alan Peck; *Ma'aserot*, Martin Jaffee; *Ma'aser Sheni*, Peter Haas; *Hallah*, Roni Herstik. The others in that Order will soon find their commentators within the present framework.

CHAPTER 13
Some Consequences of Theory: Religion and Society in Ancient Judaism with Special Reference to the Second and Third Centuries

A scholar's journey moves in ever-widening circles, down familiar paths toward frontiers of knowledge and across. For the study of religion in general, and Judaism as an example of the general, Max Weber laid out one road from the known even to the outer bounds of understanding. We do well again and again to walk on the road he laid out. There are two points of interest today in Weber's thought, one which serves to define my problem, and the other which shows the way in which I propose to solve it. First, Weber's interest in the relation between social stratification and religious ideas presents an enduring perspective for the analysis of the place of religion in society and of the relationship between religion and society. Second, Weber's mode of formulating ideal types for the purposes of analysis provides a model for how we may think about the castes, professions, and classes of society and the religious ideas they hold. The former is the fundamental issue. If we ask about whether we may discern congruence between the religious ideas to be assigned to a given group, described in gross terms as an ideal type, in ancient Israelite society, and the class status of that group, we use a mode of thought shaped by Weber in the analysis of a question raised by Weber.

It is in that sense alone that we revisit Weber. I do not propose to enrich the vast literature of interpretation of his writings, let alone discuss the enduring or transient value of his work on ancient Judaism, which is important only in the study of Weber. I shall simply take the road laid out by Weber, in order to cross frontiers of problems of interpretation not known to the world of learning in the time of Weber's *Ancient Judaism*, I mean, describing and explaining the character of Judaism as it took shape in the later first and second centuries. My purpose, stated simply, is to explore that paramount theme in Weber's great work, as expressed by Reinhard Bendix:

> In order to understand the stability and dynamics of a society we should attempt to understand these efforts in relation to the ideas and values that are prevalent in the society; or, conversely, for every given idea or value that we observe we should seek out the status group whose material and ideal way of life it tends to enhance. Thus, Weber approached the study of religious ideas in terms of their relevance for collective actions, and specially in terms of the social processes whereby the inspirations of a few become the convictions of the many. [Reinhard Bendix, *Max Weber. An Intellectual Portrait* (N.Y.: Doubleday, 1962), p. 259.]

The question then is how to relate the religious ideas held by an important group of Jews in the later first and second centuries to the social world imagined by that group.

The group under discussion is that handful of sages who, from before 70, through the period between the second war against Rome, in 132–135, and down to the end of the second century, worked out the principal themes of Israelite life and law and produced the Mishnah, their systematic account of the way in which Israel, the Jewish people in the Holy Land, should construct its life.[1] Taking up, in succession, the holiness of the Land, the proper conduct of cult and home on holy days, the holiness of family life with special reference to the transfer of women from the father's house to the husband's bed, the stable conduct of civil life, the conduct of the cult on ordinary days, and the bounds of holiness in a world of cultic uncleanness, the Mishnah designed the formative categories of reality and designated their contents.

Our work is to generalize about fundamental religious perspectives and collective actions. Now it is not difficult to take up one teaching or another within that law code and speculate about who may have said it, for what material or ideal purpose, and as an expression of which social status or context. But that sort of unsystematic and unmethodical speculation is hardly worthy of the question presented to us by Max Weber, because in the end the answers are beside the point. We wish to ask how and why "the inspirations of a few"—the sages of the document under discussion and the people who stand behind the

---

[1] Weber's formulation of the problem—the relationship of religious ideas to the group which held them—justifies our concentrating on a given book of the character of the Mishnah. First, we assume only that the Mishnah speaks for its authorities, with no presuppositions, at this point, about their prospective audience. Second, since the Mishnah to begin with is a collective document, carefully effacing the signs of individual authorship or authority, we are justified in deeming it to speak for a group. Third, as we shall now see, the Mishnah most certainly is a corpus of religious conceptions, framed, in some measure, through the medium of civil law to be sure. So it would be wrong to suppose that at hand is an exercise in treating a book as a religious community(!). Within the framework of Weber's paradigm, the Mishnah constitutes an ideal program for description and analysis of one suggestive aspect of the relationship between religion and society.

SOME CONSEQUENCES OF THEORY 115

document—become "the convictions of the many." For that purpose, episodic speculation on discrete sayings is not really pertinent, even if it *were* to be subject to the controls and tests of verification and falsification.

Rather I wish to turn to a more fundamental matter, which is the mode of thought of the group as a whole. That mode of thought is revealed, in particular, in the way in which questions are formulated. For what is telling is the asking; what is revealing is how people define what they wish to know. If we may discover the key to the system by which questions are generated and by which the logic for forming and answering those questions is made to appear to be self-evident, and if we may then relate that mode of logic and inquiry to its social setting, then I believe we may claim to speak to that program of thought laid forth by Weber in his effort "to analyze the relation between social stratification and religious ideas" (Bendix, p. 258). In this regard, individual ideas, let alone the ideas of individual thinkers, are not important. The great classical historian, Harold Cherniss, says, "The historian is concerned to comprehend the individuality of a work of art only in order that he may eliminate it and so extract for use as historical evidence those elements which are not the creation of the author" (Harold Cherniss, "The Biographical Fashion in Literary Criticism," *University of California Publications in Classical Philology*, ed. by J. T. Allen, W. H. Alexander, and G. M. Calhoun. Vol. XII, No. 15, pp. 279–92; quotation, pp. 279–80). We must do the same. That is, we are not helped to know the ideas of individuals or even the concrete and specific doctrines of the document. We wish, rather, to eliminate not only individuality, but also all specificity. So we turn to what is most general. That is, as I said, we want to discover the systemic motive behind asking a question, the power which generates and defines both problems and the logic by which they will be solved.

Let me now state the proposition of this lecture at the outset. The issues which occupy the Mishnah's philosophical mode of forming ideas and defining questions to be taken up will be seen to emerge from the social circumstance of the people of Israel in the Land of Israel. Specifically, the Mishnah's systematic preoccupation with sorting out uncertainties, with pointing up and resolving points of conflict, and with bringing into alignment contradictory principles, corresponds in thought to the confusion and doubt which then disordered Israelite social existence in the aftermath of defeat and catastrophe. In every line the Mishnah both expresses the issue of confusion in the wake of the end of the old mode of ordering life above and below, and also imposes order by sorting out confused matters. The Mishnaic message is that Israel's will is decisive. What the Israelite proposes is what disposes of questions, resolves conflict, settles doubt. Everything depends upon Israelite will, whether this thing of which we speak be expressed in terms of wish, intention, attitude, hope, conception, idea, aspiration, or other words which speak of parts of the whole entity of heart and mind. So the medium is a sequence of problems of conflict and confusion, and the message is that things are what you will them to be. In a moment of deep despair and doubt such as the later first and second centuries, this appeal to the heart and mind of Israel penetrated to the depths of the dilemma.

I
The Mishnah in its Social Setting

The Mishnah presents a "Judaism," that is, a coherent world-view and comprehensive way of living. It is a world-view which speaks of transcendent things, a way of life expressive of the supernatural meaning of what is done, a heightened and deepened perception of the sanctification of Israel in deed and in deliberation. Sanctification means two things: first, distinguishing Israel in all its dimensions from the world in all its ways; second, establishing the stability, order, regularity, predictability, and reliability of Israel at moments and in contexts of danger, meaning instability, disorder, irregularity, uncertainty, and betrayal. Each topic of the Mishnah's system of Judaism as a whole takes up a critical and indispensable moment or context of social being. Through what is said in regard to each of the Mishnah's principal topics, what the system as a whole wishes to declare is fully expressed. Yet if the parts both severally and jointly give the message of the whole, the whole cannot exist without all of the parts, so well-joined and carefully crafted are they all together.

The critical issue in economic life, which means, in farming, is in two parts. First, Israel, as tenant on God's holy Land, maintains the property in the ways God requires, keeping the rules which mark the Land and its crops as holy. Second, at the hour at which the sanctification of the Land comes to form a critical mass, namely, in the ripened crops, comes the moment ponderous with danger and heightened holiness. Israel's will so affects the crops as to mark a part of them holy, the rest of them as available for common use. The human will is determinative in the process of sanctification. Second, what happens in the Land at certain times, at Appointed Times, marks off spaces of the Land as holy in yet another way. The center of the Land

and the focus of its sanctification is the Temple. There the produce of the Land is received and given back to God, the One who created and sanctified the Land. At these unusual moments of sanctification, the inhabitants of the Land in their social being in villages enter a state of spatial sanctification. This is expressed in two ways. First, the Temple itself observes and expresses the special, recurring holy time. Second, the villages of the Land are brought into alignment with the Temple, forming a complement and completion to the Temple's sacred being. The advent of the Appointed Times precipitates a spatial reordering of the Land, so that the boundaries of the sacred are matched and mirrored in village and in Temple. At the heightened holiness marked by these moments of Appointed Times, therefore, the occasion for an affective sanctification is worked out. Like the harvest, the advent of an appointed time, a pilgrim festival, also a sacred season, is made to express that regular, orderly, and predictable sort of sanctification for Israel which the system as a whole seeks.

If for a moment we bypass the next two divisions, we come to the counterpart of the divisions of Agriculture and Appointed Times, that is, Holy Things and Purities. These divisions deal with the everyday and the ordinary, as against the special moments of harvest, on the one side, and special time or season, on the other. The Temple, the locus of continuous, as against special, sanctification, is conducted in a wholly routine and trustworthy, punctilious manner. The one thing which may unsettle matters is the intention and will of the human actor. The division of Holy Things generates its companion, the one on cultic cleanness, Purities. The relationship between the two is like that between Agriculture and Appointed Times, the former locative, the latter utopian, the former dealing with the fields, the latter with the interplay between fields and altar. Here too, once we speak of the one place of the Temple, we address, too, the cleanness which pertains to every place. A system of cleanness, taking into account what imparts uncleanness and how this is done, what is subject to uncleanness, and how that state is overcome—that system is fully expressed, once more, in response to the participation of the human will. Without the wish and act of a human being, the system does not function. It is inert. Sources of uncleanness, which come naturally and not by volition, and modes of purification, which work naturally and not by human intervention, remain inert until human will has imparted susceptibility to uncleanness, that is, introduced into the system, that food and drink, bed, pot, chair, and pan, which to begin with form the focus of the system. The movement from sanctification to uncleanness takes place when human will and work precipitate it.

The middle divisions, the third and fourth, on Women, on family law, and Damages, on civil law, finally, take their place in the structure of the whole by showing the congruence, within the larger framework of sanctification through regularity and the perfection of social order, of human concerns of family and farm, politics and workaday transactions among ordinary people. For without attending to these matters, the Mishnah's system does not encompass what, at its foundations, it is meant to comprehend and order. What is at issue is fully cogent with the rest. In the case of Women, attention focuses upon the point of disorder marked by the transfer of that disordering anomaly, woman, from the regular status provided by one man, to the equally trustworthy status provided by another. That is the point at which the Mishnah's interests are aroused: once more, predictably, the moment of disorder. In the case of Damages, there are two important concerns. First, there is the paramount interest in preventing, so far as possible, the disorderly rise of one person and fall of another, and in sustaining the *status quo* of the economy of the household of Israel, the holy society in perfect stasis. Second, there is the necessary concomitant in the provision of a system of political institutions to carry out the laws which preserve the balance and steady state of persons.

The divisions which take up topics of concrete and material concern, the formation and dissolution of families and the transfer of property in that connection, the transactions, both through torts and through commerce, which lead to exchanges of property and the potential dislocation of the state of families in society, are both locative and utopian. They deal with the concrete locations in which people make their lives, household and street and field, the sexual and commerical exchanges of a given village. But they pertain to the life of all Israel, both in the Land and otherwise. These two divisions, together with the household ones of Appointed Times, constitute the sole opening outward toward the life of utopian Israel, that diaspora in the far reaches of the ancient world. This community from the Mishnah's perspective is not merely in exile, but unaccounted for; it is simply outside the system, for the Mishnah declines to recognize and take it into account. Israelites who dwell in the land of (unclean) death instead of in the Land simply fall outside the realm and range of (holy) life.

If we ask ourselves about the sponsorship and source of special interest in the topics just now reviewed, we come up with obvious answers.

So far as the Mishnah is a document about the holiness of Israel in its Land, it expresses that conception of sanctification and theory of its mode which will have been shaped among those to whom the Temple and its technology of joining Heaven and holy Land through the sacred place defined the core of being, I mean, the caste of the priests.

So far as the Mishnah takes up the way in which transactions are conducted among ordinary folk and takes the position that it is through documents that transactions are embodied and expressed (surely the position of the relevant tractates on both Women and Damages), the Mishnah expresses what is self-evident to scribes. Just as, to the priest, there is a correspondence between the table of the Lord in the Temple and the locus of the divinity in the heavens, so, to the scribe, there is a correspondence between the documentary expression of the human will on earth, in writs of all sorts, in the orderly provision of courts for the predictable and just disposition of exchanges of persons and property, and Heaven's judgment of these same matters. When a woman becomes sanctified to a particular man on earth, through the appropriate document governing the transfer of her person and property, in heaven as well, the woman is deemed truly sanctified to that man. A violation of the writ therefore is not merely a crime. It is a sin. That is why the Temple rite involving the wife accused of adultery is integral to the system of the division of Women.

So there are these two social groups, but they are not symmetrical with one another. For one is the priestly caste, and the other is the scribal profession. We know, moreover, that in time to come, the profession would become a focus of sanctification too. The scribe would be transformed into the rabbi, locus of the holy through what he knew, just as the priest had been, and would remain, locus of the holy through what he could claim for genealogy. The tractates of special interest to scribes-become-rabbis and to their governance of Israelite society, those of Women and Damages, together with certain others particularly relevant to utopian Israel beyond the system of the Land—those tractates would grow and grow. Others would remain essentially as they were with the closure of the Mishnah. So we must notice that the Mishnah, for its part, speaks about the program of topics important to the priests. It does so in the persona of the scribes, speaking through their voice and in their manner.

Now what we do not find is astonishing in the light of these observations. It is sustained and serious attention to the matter of the caste of the priests and of the profession of the scribes. True, scattered through the tractates are exercises, occasionally important exercises, on the genealogy of the priestly caste, their marital obligations and duties, as well as on the things priests do and do not do in the cult, in collecting and eating their sanctified food, and other topics of keen interest to priests. Indeed, it would be no exaggeration to say that the Mishnah's system, seen whole, is not a great deal more than a handbook of how the priestly caste wished to design its life in Israel and the world. And this is what makes amazing the fact that in the fundamental structure of the document, its organization into divisions and tractates, there is no place for a division of the Priesthood. There is no room even for a complete tractate on the rules of the priesthood, except, as we have seen, for the pervasive way of life of the priestly caste, which is everywhere. This absence of sustained attention to the priesthood is striking, when we compare the way in which the Priestly Code at Leviticus Chapters One through Fifteen spells out its triplet of concerns: the priesthood, the cult, the matter of cultic cleanness. Since we have divisions for the cult and for cleanness at Holy Things and Purities, we are struck by the absence of a parallel to the third division.

We must, moreover, be equally surprised that, for a document so rich in the importance lent to petty matters of how a writ is folded and where the witnesses sign, so obsessed with the making of long lists and the organization of all knowledge into neat piles of symmetrically arranged words, the scribes who know how to make lists and match words nowhere come to the fore. They speak through the document, but they stand behind the curtains. They write the script, arrange the sets, design the costumes, situate the players in their place on the stage, raise the curtain—and play no role at all. We have no division or tractate on such matters as how a person becomes a scribe, how a scribe conducts his work, who forms the center of the scribal profession and how authority is gained therein, the rights and place of the scribe in the system of governance through courts, the organization and conduct of schools or circles of masters and disciples through which the scribal arts are taught and perpetuated. This absence of even minimal information on the way in which the scribal profession takes shape and does its work is stunning, when we realize that, within a brief generation, the Mishnah as a whole would fall into the hands of scribes, called rabbis,[2] both in the Land of Israel and in Babylonia. These rabbis would make of the Mishnah exactly what they wished. Construed from the perspective of the makers of the Mishnah, the priests and the scribes who provide contents and form, substance and style, therefore, the Mishnah turns out to omit all reference to actors, when laying out the world which is their play.

---

[2] But the title, "rabbi," cannot be thought particular to those who served as judges and administrators in small-claims courts and as scribes and authorities in the Jewish community, called "rabbis" in Talmudic literature and afterward. The title is clearly prior to its particularization in the institutions of the Talmudic community.

SOME CONSEQUENCES OF THEORY 121

The metaphor of the theater for the economy of Israel, the household of holy Land and people, space and time, cult and home, leads to yet another perspective. When we look out upon the vast drama portrayed by the Mishnah, lacking as it does an account of the one who wrote the book, and the one about whom the book was written, we notice yet one more missing component. In the fundamental and generative structure of the Mishnah, we find no account of that other necessary constituent: the audience. To whom the document speaks is never specified. What group ("class") generates the Mishnah's problems is not at issue. True, it is taken for granted that the world of the Mishnah expresses the sanctified being of Israel in general. So the Mishnah speaks about the generality of Israel, the people. But to whom, within Israel, the Mishnah addresses itself, and what groups are expected to want to know what the Mishnah has to say are matters which never come to full expression.

There can be no doubt of the answer to the question. The building block of Mishnaic discourse, the circumstance addressed whenever the issues of concrete society and material transactions are taken up, is the householder and his context. The Mishnah knows all sorts of economic activities, but for the Mishnah the center and focus of interest lie in the village. The village is made up of households, each a unit of production in farming. The households are constructed by, and around, the householder, father of an extended family, including his sons and their wives and children, his servants, his slaves, the craftsmen to whom he entrusts tasks he does not choose to do. The concerns of householders are in transactions in land. Their measurement of value is expressed in acreage of top, middle, and bottom grade. Through real estate critical transactions are worked out. The marriage settlement depends upon real property. Civil penalties are extracted through payment of real property. The principal transactions to be taken up are those of the householder who owns beasts which do damage or suffer it; who harvests his crops and must set aside and so by his own word and deed sanctify them for use by the castes scheduled from on high; who uses or sells his crops and feeds his family; and who, if he is fortunate, will acquire still more land. It is to householders that the Mishnah is addressed: the pivot of society and its bulwark, the units of production of which the village is composed, the corporate component of the society of Israel in the limits of the village and the land. The householder, as I said, is the building block of the house of Israel, of its *economy* in the classic sense of the word.

To revert to the metaphor which has served us well, the great proscenium constructed by the Mishnah now looms before us. Its arch is the canopy of heaven. Its stage is the holy Land of Israel, corresponding to heaven. Its actors are the holy people of Israel. Its events are the drama of unfolding time and common transactions, appointed times and holy events. Yet in this grand design we look in vain for the three principal participants: the audience, the actors, and the playwright. So we must ask why.

The reason is not difficult to discover, when we recall that, after all, what the Mishnah really wants is for nothing to happen. The Mishnah presents a tableau, a wax museum, a diorama. It portrays a world fully perfected and so wholly at rest. The one thing the Mishnah does not want to tell us about is change, how things come to be, or cease to be, what they are. That is why there can be no sustained attention to the caste of the priesthood and its rules, the scribal profession and its constitution, the class of householders and its interests. The Mishnah's pretense is that all of these have come to rest. They compose a world in stasis, perfect and complete, made holy because it is complete and perfect. It is an economy—again in the classic sense of the word—awaiting the divine *act* of sanctification which, as at the creation of the world, would set the seal of holy rest upon an again-complete creation, just as in the beginning. There is no place for the actors when what is besought is not action whatsoever, but only perfection, which is unchanging. There is room only for a description of how things are: the present tense, the sequence of completed statements and static problems. All the action lies within, in how these statements are made. Once they come to full expression, with nothing left to say, there also is nothing left to do, no need for actors, whether scribes, priests, or householders.

We have now to ask how the several perspectives joined in the Mishnah do coalesce. What that single message is which brings them all together, and how that message forms a powerful, if transient, catalyst for the social groups which hold it—these define the task in portraying the Judaism for which the Mishnah is the whole evidence. Integral to that task is an account of why, for the moment, the catalyst could serve, as it clearly did, to join together diverse agents, to mingle, mix, indeed, unite, for a fleeting moment, social elements quite unlike one another, indeed not even capable of serving as analogies for one another.

One of the paramount, recurring exercises of the Mishnaic thinkers is to give an account of how things which are different from one another become part of one another, that is, the problem of mixtures. This problem of mixtures will be in many dimensions, involving cases of doubt; cases of shared traits and distinctive ones; cases of confusion of essentially distinct elements and components; and numerous other concrete instances of successful and of unsuccessful, complete and partial catalysis. If I had to choose one prevailing motif of Mishnaic thought, it is this: the joining together of categories which are distinct, the distinguishing among those which are confused. The Mishnaic mode of thought is to bring together principles and to show both how they conflict and how the conflict is resolved; to deal with gray areas and to lay down principles for disposing of cases of doubt; to take up the analysis of entities into their component parts and the catalysis of distinct substances into a single entity; to analyze the whole, to synthesize the parts. The motive force behind the Mishnah's intellectual program of cases and examples, the thing the authorship of the Mishnah wants to do with all of the facts it has in its hand, is described within this inquiry into mixtures. Now the reasons for this deeply typical, intellectual concern with confusion and order, I think, are probably to be found here and there and everywhere.

For, after all, the basic mode of thought of the priests who made up the priestly Creation-legend (Gen 1:1–2:4a), is that creation is effected through the orderly formation of each thing after its kind and correct location of each in its place. The persistent quest of the Mishnaic subsystems is for stasis, order, the appropriate situation of all things.

A recurrent theme in the philosophical tradition of Greco-Roman antiquity, current in the time of the Mishnah's formative intellectual processes, is the nature of mixtures,[3] the interpenetration of distinct substances and their qualities, the juxtaposition of incomparables. The types of mixture were themselves organized in a taxonomy: a mechanical composition, in which the components remain essentially unchanged, a total fusion, in which all particles are changed and lose their individual properties, and, in between, a mixture proper, in which there is a blending. So concern for keeping things straight and in their place is part of the priestly heritage, and it also is familiar to the philosophical context in which scribes can have had their being. Nor will the householders have proved disinterested in the notion of well-marked borders and stable and dependable frontiers between different things. What was to be fenced in and fenced out hardly requires specification.

And yet, however tradition and circumstances may have dictated this point of interest in mixtures and their properties, in sorting out what is confused and finding a proper place for every thing, I think

---

[3] I refer to S. Samburksy, *The Physics of the Stoics*.

there is still another reason for the recurrence of a single type of exercise and a uniform mode of thought. It is the social foundation for the intellectual exercise which is the Mishnah and its Judaism. In my view the very condition of Israel, standing, at the end of the second century, on the limns of its own history, at the frontiers among diverse peoples, on both sides of every boundary, whether political or cultural or intellectual—it is the condition of Israel itself which attracted attention to this matter of sorting things out. *The concern for the catalyst which joins what is originally distinct, the powerful attraction of problems of confusion and chaos, on the one side, and order and form, on the other—these form the generative problematic of the Mishnah as a system because they express in intellectual form the very nature and essential being of Israel in its social condition at that particular moment in Israel's history.* It is therefore the profound congruence of the intellectual program and the social and historical realities taken up and worked out by that intellectual program which accounts for the power of the Mishnah to define the subsequent history of Judaism. That is why the inspirations of the few in time would become the convictions of the many. It is what Weber's questions generate for answers.

II

The Mishnah's Methods of Thought

Now that the tributaries to the Mishnah have been specified, we have to turn to those traits of style and substance in which the Mishnah vastly exceeds the flood of its tributaries, becomes far more than the sum of its parts. The Mishnah in no way presents itself as a document of class, caste, or profession. It is something different. The difference comes to complete statement in the two dimensions which mark the measure of any work of intellect: style and substance, mode of thought, medium of expression, and message. These have now to be specified with full attention to recurrent patterns to be discerned among the myriad of detailed rules, problems, and exercises, of which the Mishnah is composed.[4]

Let us take up, first of all, the matter of style. The Mishnah's paramount literary trait is its emphasis on disputes about the law. Nearly all disputes, which dominate the rhetoric of the Mishnah, derive from bringing diverse legal principles into formal juxtaposition and

---

[4] Documentation for the general statements made in this section will be found in my *Judaism: The Evidence of the Mishnah* (Chicago: The University of Chicago Press, 1981).

substantive conflict. So we may say that the Mishnah as a whole is an exercise in the application to a given case, through practical reason, of several distinct and conflicting principles of law. In this context, it follows, the Mishnah is a protracted inquiry into the intersection of principles. It maps out the gray areas of the law delimited by such limns of confusion. An example of this type of "mixture" of legal principles comes in the conflict of two distinct bodies of the law. But gray areas are discerned not only through mechanical juxtaposition, making up a conundrum of distinct principles of law. On the contrary, the Mishnaic philosophers are at their best when they force into conflict laws which, to begin with, scarcely intersect. This they do, for example, by inventing cases in which the secondary implications of one law are brought into conflict with the secondary implications of some other. Finally, nothing will so instantly trigger the imagination of the Mishnah's exegetical minds as matters of ambiguity. A species of the genus of gray areas of the law is the excluded middle, that is, that creature or substance which appears to fall between two distinct and definitive categories. The Mishnah's framers time and again allude to such an entity, because it forms the excluded middle which inevitably will attract attention and demand categorization. There are types of recurrent middles among both human beings and animals as well as vegetables. Indeed, the obsession with the excluded middle leads the Mishnah to invent its own examples, which have then to be analyzed into their definitive components and situated in their appropriate category. What this does is to leave no area lacking in an appropriate location, none to yield irresoluble doubt.

The purpose of identifying the excluded middle is to allow the lawyers to sort out distinct rules, on the one side, and to demonstrate how they intersect without generating intolerable uncertainty, on the other. For example, to explore the theory that an object can serve as either a utensil or a tent, that is, a place capable of spreading the uncleanness of a corpse under its roof, the framers of the Mishnah invent a "hive." This is sufficiently large so that it can be imagined to be either a utensil or a tent. When it is whole, it is the former, and if it is broken, it is the latter. The location of the object, e.g., on the ground, off the ground, in a doorway, against a wall, and so on, will further shape the rules governing the cases (M. Ohalot 9:1–14). Again, to indicate the ambiguities lying at the frontiers, the topic of the status of Syria will come under repeated discussion. Syria is deemed not wholly sanctified, as is the Land of Israel, but also not wholly outside of the frame of holy Land, as are all other countries. That is why to Syria apply some rules applicable to holy Land, some rules applicable to secular land. In consequence, numerous points of ambiguity will be uncovered and explored (M. Sheb. 6:1-6).

Gray areas of the law in general, and the excluded middle in particular, cover the surface of the law. They fill up nearly every chapter of the Mishnah. But underneath the surface is an inquiry of profound and far-reaching range. It is into the metaphysical or philosophical issues of how things join together, and how they do not, of synthesis and analysis, of fusion and union, connection, division and disintegration. What we have in the recurrent study of the nature of mixtures, broadly construed, is a sustained philosophical treatise in the guise of an episodic exercise in *ad hoc* problem-solving. It is as if the cultic agendum, laid forth by the priests, the social agendum, defined by the confusing status and condition of Israel, and the program for right categorization of persons and things, set forth for the scribes to carry out—all were taken over and subsumed by the philosophers who proposed to talk abstractly about what they deemed urgent, while using the concrete language and syntax of untrained minds. To put it differently, the framers of the Mishnah, in their reflection on the nature of mixtures in their various potentialities for formation and dissolution, shape into hidden discourse, on an encompassing philosophical-physical problem of their own choosing, topics provided by others.

In so doing, they phrased the critical question demanding attention and response, the question in dimensions at once social, political, metaphysical, cultural, and even linguistic, but above all, historical: the question of Israel, standing at the outer boundaries of a long history now decisively done with. That same question of acculturation and assimilation, alienation and exile, which had confronted the sixth century B.C. priests of the Priestly Code from 70 to 200 was raised once more. Now it is framed in terms of mechanical composition, fusion, and something in between, mixture. But it is phrased in incredible terms of a wildly irrelevant world of unseen things, of how we define the place of the stem in the entity of the apple, the affect of the gravy upon the meat, and the definitive power of a bit of linen in a fabric of wool. In concrete form, the issues are close to comic. In abstract form, the answers speak of nothing of workaday meaning. In reality, at issue is Israel in its Land, once the lines of structure which had emanated from the Temple had been blurred and obliterated. It is in this emphasis upon sorting out confused things that the Mishnah becomes truly Mishnaic, distinct from modes of thought and perspective to be assigned to groups represented in the document. To interpret the meaning of this emphasis, we must again recall that the Priestly Code makes the point that a well-ordered society on earth, with its center and point of reference at the Temple altar, corresponds to a well-ordered canopy of heaven. Creation comes to its climax at the perfect rest marked by completion and signifying perfection and sanctification. Indeed, the creation-myth represents as the occasion for sanctification a perfected world at rest, with all things in their rightful place. Now the Mishnah takes up this conviction, which is located at the deepest structures of the metaphysic of the framers of the Priestly Code and, therefore, of their earliest continuators and imitators in the Mishnaic code. But the Mishnah does not frame the conviction that in order is salvation through a myth of creation and a description of a cult of precise and perfect order, such as is at Gen 1:1–2:4a. True, the Mishnah imposes order upon the world through lines of structure emanating from the cult. The verses of Scripture selected as authoritative leave no alternative.

The Mishnah at its deepest layers, however, taking up the raw materials of concern of priests and farmers and scribes, phrases that concern after the manner of philosophers. That is to say, the framers of the Mishnah speak of the physics of mixtures, conflicts of principles which must be sorted out, areas of doubt generated by confusion. The detritus of a world seeking order but suffering chaos now is reduced to the construction of intellect. If, therefore, we wish to characterize the Mishnah when it is cogent and distinctive, we must point to this persistent and pervasive mode of thought. For the Mishnah takes up a vast corpus of facts and treats these facts, so to speak, "Mishnaically," that is, in a way distinctive to the Mishnah, predictable and typical of the Mishnah. That is what I mean when I refer to the style of the Mishnah: its manner of exegesis of a topic, its mode of thought about any subject, the sorts of perplexities which will precipitate the Mishnah's fertilizing flood of problem-making ingenuity. Confusion and conflict will trigger the Mishnah's power to control conflict by showing its limits, and, thus, the range of shared conviction too.

For by treating the facts "Mishnaically," the Mishnah establishes boundaries around, and pathways through, confusion. It lays out roads to guide people by ranges of permissible doubt. Consequently, the Mishnah's mode of control over the chaos of conflicting principles, the confusion of doubt, the improbabilities of a world out of alignment, is to delimit and demarcate. By exploring the range of interstitial conflict through its ubiquitous disputes, the Mishnah keeps conflict under control. It so preserves that larger range of agreement, that pervasive and shared conviction, which is never expressed, which is always instantiated, and which, above all, is forever taken for granted. The

Mishnah's deepest convictions about what lies beyond confusion and conflict are never spelled out; they lie in the preliminary, unstated exercise prior to the commencement of a sustained exercise of inquiry, a tractate. They are the things we know before we take up that exercise and study that tractate.

All of this vast complex of methods and styles, some of them intellectual, some of them literary and formal, may be captured in the Mishnah's treatment of its own, self-generated conflicts of principles, its search for gray areas of the law. It also may be clearly discerned in the Mishnah's sustained interest in those excluded middles it makes up for the purpose of showing the limits of the law, the confluence and conflict of laws. It further may be perceived in the Mishnah's recurrent exercise in the study of types of mixtures, the ways distinct components of an entity may be joined together, may be deemed separate from one another, may be shown to be fused, or may be shown to share some traits and not others. Finally, the Mishnah's power to sort out matters of confusion will be clearly visible in its repeated statement of the principles by which cases of doubt are to be resolved. A survey of these four modes of thought thus shows us one side of the distinctive and typical character of the Mishnah, when the Mishnah transcends the program of facts, forms, and favored perspectives of its tributaries. We now turn to the side of substance. What causes and resolves confusion and chaos is the power of the Israelite's will. As is said in the context of measurements for minimum quantities to be subject to uncleanness, "All accords with the measure of the man" (M. Kel. 17:11).

The Mishnah's principal message is that Israelite man is at the center of creation, the head of all creatures upon earth, corresponding to God in heaven, in whose image man is made. The way in which the Mishnah makes this simple and fundamental statement is to impute power to the Israelite to inaugurate and initiate those corresponding processes, sanctification and uncleanness, which play so critical a role in the Mishnah's account of reality. The will of man, expressed through the deed of man, is the active power in the world. Will and deed— these constitute those actors of creation which work upon neutral realms, subject to either sanctification or uncleanness: the Temple and table, the field and family, the altar and hearth, woman, time, space, transactions in the material world and in the world above as well. An object, a substance, a transaction, even a phrase or a sentence, is inert but may be made holy, when the interplay of the will and deed of man arouses and generates its potential to be sanctified. Each may be treated as ordinary or (where relevant) made unclean by neglect of the will and inattentive act of man. Just as the entire system of uncleanness and holiness awaits the intervention of man, which imparts the capacity to become unclean upon what was formerly inert, or which removes the capacity to impart cleanness from what was formerly in its natural and puissant condition, so in the other ranges of reality, man is at the center on earth, just as is God in heaven. Man is counterpart and partner in creation, in that, like God he has power over the status and condition of creation, putting everything in its proper place, calling everything by its rightful name.

So, stated briefly, the question taken up by the Mishnah is, What can a man do? And the answer laid down by the Mishnah is, Man, through will and deed, is master of this world, the measure of all things. Since when the Mishnah thinks of man, it means the Israelite, who is the subject and actor of its system, the statement is clear. This man is Israel, who can do what he wills. In the aftermath of the two wars, the message of the Mishnah cannot have proved more pertinent—or poignant and tragic. The principal message of the Mishnah is that the will of man affects the material reality of the world and governs the working of those forces, visible or not, which express and effect the sanctification of creation and of Israel alike. This message comes to the surface in countless ways. At the outset a simple example of the supernatural power of man's intention suffices to show the basic power of the Israelite's will to change concrete, tangible facts. The power of the human will is nowhere more effective than in the cult, where, under certain circumstances, what a person is thinking is more important than what he does. The basic point is that if an animal is designated for a given purpose, but the priest prepares the animal with the thought in mind that the beast serves some other sacrificial purpose, then, in some instances, in particular involving a sin offering and a Passover on the fourteenth of Nisan, the sacrifice is ruined. In this matter of preparation of the animal, moreover, are involved the deeds of slaughtering the beast, collecting, conveying, and tossing the blood on the altar, that is, the principal priestly deeds of sacrifice. Again, if the priest has in mind, when doing these deeds, to offer up the parts to be offered up on the altar, or to eat the parts to be eaten by the priest, in some location other than the proper one (the altar, the courtyard, respectively), or at some time other than the requisite one (the next few hours), the rite is spoiled, the meat must be thrown out. Now that is the case, even if the priest did not do what he was thinking of doing. Here again we have a testimony to the fundamental importance imputed to what a person is thinking, even over what he actually does, in critical aspects of the holy life (M. Zebahim 1:1–4:6, Menahot 1:1–4:5).

Once man wants something, a system of the law begins to function. Intention has the power, in particular, to initiate the processes of sanctification. The moment at which something becomes sacred and so falls under a range of severe penalties for misappropriation or requires a range of strict modes of attentiveness and protection for the preservation of cleanness is defined by the human will. Stated simply: at the center of the Mishnaic system is the notion that man has the power to inaugurate the work of sanctification, and the Mishnaic system states and restates that power. This assessment of the positive power of the human will begins with the matter of uncleanness, one antonym of sanctification or holiness. Man alone has the power to inaugurate the system of uncleanness.

From the power of man to introduce an object or substance into the processes of uncleanness, we turn to the corresponding power of man to sanctify an object or a substance. This is a much more subtle matter, but it also is more striking. It is the act of designation by a human being which "activates" that holiness inherent in crops from which no tithes have yet been set aside and removed. Once the human being has designated what is holy within the larger crop, then that designated portion of the crop gathers within itself the formerly-diffused holiness and becomes holy, set aside for the use and benefit of the priest to whom it is given. So it is the interplay between the will of the farmer, who owns the crop, and the sanctity inherent in the whole batch of the crop itself, which is required for the processes of sanctification to work themselves out.

In addition to the power to initiate the process of sanctification and the system of uncleanness and cleanness, man has the power, through the working of his will, to differentiate one thing from another. The fundamental category into which an entity, which may be this or that, is to be placed is decided by the human will for that entity. Man exercises the power of categorization, so ends confusion. Once more, the consequence will be that, what man decides, Heaven confirms or ratifies. Once man determines that something falls into one category and not another, the interest of Heaven is provoked. Then misuse of that thing invokes Heavenly penalties. Man's will has the capacity so to work as to engage the ratifying power of Heaven. Let us take up first of all the most striking example, the deed itself. It would be difficult to doubt that what one does determines the effect of what one does. But that position is rejected. The very valence and result of a deed depend, to begin with, on one's prior intent. The intent which leads a person to do a deed governs the culpability of the deed. There is no intrinsic weight to the deed itself. Human will not only is definitive. It also provides the criterion for differentiation in cases of uncertainty or doubt. This is an overriding fact. That is why I insisted earlier that the principal range of questions addressed by the Mishnah—areas of doubt and uncertainty about status or taxonomy—provokes an encompassing response. This response, it now is clear, in the deep conviction of the Mishnaic law, present at the deepest structures of the law, is that what man wills or thinks decides all issues of taxonomy.

To conclude: The characteristic mode of thought of the Mishnah thus is to try to sort things out, exploring the limits of conflict and the range of consensus. The one thing which the Mishnah's framers predictably want to know concerns what falls between two established categories or rules, the gray area of the law, the excluded middle among entities, whether persons, places, or things. This obsession with the liminal or marginal comes to its climax and fulfillment in the remarkably wide-ranging inquiry into the nature of mixtures, whether these are mixtures of substances in a concrete framework or of principles and rules in an abstract one. So the question is fully phrased by both the style of the Mishnaic discourse and its rhetoric. It then is fully answered. The question of how we know what something is, the way in which we assign to its proper frame and category what crosses the lines between categories, is settled by what Israelite man wants, thinks, hopes, believes, and how he so acts as to indicate his attitude. With the question properly phrased in the style and mode of Mishnaic thought and discourse, the answer is not difficult to express. What makes the difference, what sets things into their proper category and resolves those gray areas of confusion and conflict formed when simple principles intersect and produce dispute, is man's will. Israel's despair or hope is the definitive and differentiating criterion.

III
The Convictions of the Many

Passionate concern for order and stability, for sorting things out and resolving confusion, ambiguity, and doubt—these may well characterize the minds of priests, scribes, and householders. The priests, after all, emerge from a tradition of sanctification achieved through the perfection of the order of creation—that is the theology of their Creation-myth. The scribes, with their concern for the correspondence between what they do on earth and what is accorded approval and confirmation in Heaven, likewise carry forward that interest in form and order characteristic of a profession of their kind. But if I had to choose that single group for whom the system speaks, it would be neither of these. We noted at the outset that the scribe and the priest are noteworthy by their absence from the fundamental structure and organization of the Mishnah's documents. By contrast, the householder forms the focus of two of the six divisions, those devoted to civil law and family. Let us then reflect for a moment on the ways in which the householder will have found the Mishnah's principal modes of concern congruent with his own program. We speak now of the householder in a courtyard, for he is the subject of most predicates. He is the proprietor of an estate, however modest. He also is a landholder in the fields, however little, an employer with a legitimate claim against lazy or unreliable workers, the head of a family, and the manager of a small but self-contained farm. He is someone who gives over his property to craftsmen for their skilled labor, but is not a craftsman himself. He also is someone with a keen interest in assessing and collecting damages done to his herds and flocks, or in paying what he must for what his beasts do. The Mishnah speaks for someone who deems thievery to be the paltry, petty thievery ("Oh! the servants!") of watchmen of an orchard and herdsmen of a flock, and for a landowner constantly involved in transactions in real property.

The Mishnah's class-perspective, described merely from its topics and problems, is that of the undercapitalized and overextended upper-class farmer, who has no appreciation whatsoever for the interests of those with liquid capital and no understanding of the role of trading in commodity-futures. This landed proprietor of an estate of some size sees a bushel of grain as a measure of value. But he does not concede that, in the provision of supplies and sustenance through the year, from one harvest to the next, lies a kind of increase no less productive than the increase of the fields and the herd. The Mishnah is the voice of the head of the household, the pillar of society, the model of the community, the arbiter and mediator of the goods of this world, fair, just, honorable, above all, reliable.

The Mishnah therefore is the voice of the Israelite landholding, proprietary class [compare *Soviet Views of Talmudic Judaism. Five Papers by Yu. A. Solodukho in English Translation*, edited with a commentary by this writer (Leiden: E. J. Brill, 1973)]. Its problems are the problems of the landowner, the householder, as I said, the Mishnah's basic and recurrent subject for nearly all predicates. Its perspectives are his. Its sense of what is just and fair expresses his sense of the givenness and cosmic rightness of the present condition of society. Earth matches Heaven. The Mishnah's hope for Heaven and its claim on earth, to earth, corresponding to the supernatural basis for the natural world, bespeak the imagination of the surviving Israelite burgherdom of the mid-second century Land of Israel—people deeply tired of war and its dislocation, profoundly distrustful of messiahs and their dangerous promises. These are men of substance and means, however modest, aching for a stable and predictable world in which to tend their crops and herds, feed their families and workers, keep to the natural rhythms of the seasons and the lunar cycles, and, in all, live out their lives within strong and secure boundaries, on earth and in Heaven.

When we turn away from the Mishnah's imagined world to the actual context of the Israelite community after the destruction of the Temple in 70 and still later after Bar Kokhba, we are able to discern what it is that the Mishnah's sages have for raw materials, the slime they have for mortar, the bricks they have for building. The archaeological evidence of the later second and third centuries reveals a thriving Israelite community in Galilee and surrounding regions, a community well able to construct for itself synagogues of considerable aesthetic ambition, to sustain and support an internal government and the appurtenances of an abundant life. What that means is that, while the south was permanently lost, the north remained essentially intact. Indeed, it would be on the sturdy and secure foundations of that stable community of the northern part of the Land of Israel that Israelite life for the next three or four hundred years—a very long time—would be constructed.

So when the Mishnah's sages cast their eyes out on the surviving Israelite world, their gaze must have rested upon that thing which had endured, and would continue to endure, beyond the unimaginable catastrophe bought on by Bar Kokhba and his disruptive messianic adventure. Extant and enduring was a world of responsible, solid farmers and their slaves and dependents, the men and women upon the backs of whom the Israelite world would now have come to rest. They, their children, slaves, dependents could yet make a world to endure—if only they could keep what they had, pretty much as they had it—no more, but also no less. Theirs was not a society aimed at aggrandizement. They wanted no more than to preserve what had survived out of the disorderly past. That is why the Mishnah's is not a system respectful of increase. It asks no more than that what is to be is to be. The Mishnah seeks the perfection of a world at rest, the precondition of that seal of creation's perfection sanctified on the seventh day of Creation and perpetually sanctified by the seventh day of Creation.

But if the philosophers of Israelite society refer to a real world, a world in being, the values of which were susceptible of protection and preservation, the boundaries of which were readily discerned, they also defied that real world. They speak of location but have none. For Israelite settlement in the Land then was certainly not contiguous. There was no polity resting on a homogeneous social basis. All Israel had were villages, on a speckled map of villages of many peoples. There was no Israelite nation, in full charge of its lands or Land, standing upon contiguous and essentially united territories. This locative polity is built upon utopia: no one place. The ultimate act of will is forming a locative system in no particular place, speaking nowhere about somewhere, concretely specifying utopia. This is done—in context—because Israel wills it.

At the end, Weber's problem points the way for further inquiry: How do the inspirations of a few become the convictions of the many? For, we observe, while the Mishnah came into the world as the lawbook of a class of scribes and small-claims-court-judges, it in time to come formed the faith and piety of the many of Israel, the Jews at large, the workers and craftsmen. And these, it must be emphasized, were not landholders and farmers. They were in the main landless craftsmen and workers, but they took over this book of landholders and farmers and accepted it as the other half, the Oral half, of the whole Torah of God to Moses at Mount Sinai.

That is to say, in somewhat less mythological terms, the Mishnah began with some one group, in fact, with a caste, a class, and a profession. But it very rapidly came to form the heart and center of the imaginative life and concrete politics, law, and society of a remarkably diverse set of groups, that is, the Jewish people as a whole. So the really interesting question, when we move from the account of Israelite religion and society in the first and second centuries, represented by the Mishnah, to religion and society in the third and fourth centuries, represented by the Talmuds, and in the fifth and later centuries represented by the Midrashim, is how the Mishnah was transformed in social context from one thing into something else. If, as I said at the outset, we locate "the status group whose material and ideal way of life a given idea or value tends to enhance," then we must ask why that same idea or value served, as it did, to enhance a far wider and more encompassing group within Israelite society. We must investigate how it came about that, in time to come, Judaism, the world-view and way of life resting upon the Scriptures and upon the Mishnah and in due course upon the Talmuds, came to constitute the world-view and way of life of nearly all Israel.

The difficult question before us is the truly historical one: the question of change, of why things begin in one place but move onward, and of how we may account for what happens. The weak point of sociology of religion, in Weber's powerful formulation, emerges from its strong point. If we begin by asking about the relevance of religious ideas to collective actions, we must proceed to wonder about the continuing relevance of religious ideas within a changing collectivity and context. If, as Bendix says, Weber emphasizes the issue of how a given idea or value enhances the way of life of a "status-group," then we must wonder why that given idea or value succeeds in maintaining its own free-standing, ongoing life among and for entirely other status-groups and types of social groups. The history of Judaism from the formation of the Mishnah onward through the next four centuries, amply documented as is that period, provides one important arena for inquiry into yet another constituent of Weber's grand program.

Part IV
Epilogue

CHAPTER 14
Judaic Studies as the Humanities of the Jewish Heritage

So far as we mean by "Jewish studies" systematic learning in the classic texts of the Jewish heritage, treating such studies as part of the humanities presents a problem. For the humanities study the character and achievement of men and women in this world. When we succeed in humanistic learning, we understand more about ourselves, our minds, imagination, emotion, and the society and culture we create. But when we succeed in Judaic studies, properly understood within their own frame of discourse, we understand more about God and what God wants of us. Let me spell this out.

That Jewish studies belong in the humanities is hardly obvious. For the more important texts of Jewish learning are religious. They are part of Torah, divine revelation. Consequently, they fall properly not into the humanities, but into "the divinities." That is to say, Judaic studies undertake the religious, not the humanistic, study of Judaism. In the beginning, after all, the human sciences, the humanities, were defined by contrast to the divine sciences; the study of humanity was defined against the study of divinity. To find a place for the study of religion within the framework of the study of humanity is the present task, part of which involves locating Jewish studies in the humanities. To define the study of humanity from the perspective of divine sciences, the task is to describe sacred images of humanity. To define the study of divinity from the perspective of the human sciences, it is to analyze human images of divinity. To state matters in the context of Judaism, the divine sciences (study of Torah) present man in God's image, and the humane sciences (religious studies), God in man's image.

The first question is what it means to engage in the humanistic study of divinity, and the second, whether such a mode of learning is authentic to the character and claim of what is studied. By this I mean that if all we wished to learn about the human being is the chemical content of the body, then I think we should ask the wrong question and produce an answer incongruous to what is studied. Chemistry is not authentic to the study of the human being. These two questions, then, urgently confront anyone who proposes to explain how Jewish studies may be described as "the humanities of the Jewish heritage."

Humanistic study of a religion, or religion as a genus of human activity, wants to know what we learn about humanity from humanity's yearning for God, devotion to supernatural revelation, dedication of this life to the life to come and vision of humanity as a sacred projection on to earth. True, the question of the humanistic study of religion reverses matters. It is, as I said, to see divinity as a secular projection on to heaven. Yet that need not be the end of the matter, for, in the tradition of Judaism at least, to know more about humanity is to understand something of the divinity. "Let us make Adam in our image," requires us to revere and stand in awe of humanity "in our likeness." It is here that the heaven and earth meet—in the study of the humanist who knows what the issues truly are.

Since the humanities encompass the study of history, literature, philosophy, art, music, and the other intangible treasures of human emotion, wisdom, and learning, the study of religion to begin with does the same. That is, we study the history, literature, philosophy, art, music that people have made because they believed in a realm beyond this one, a God beyond themselves. But not these alone have people made. More than history, literature, philosophy, they have made temples on hilltops and cities in deserts, where they should not be, cathedrals of time in space they should not occupy. Society and systems of culture, ways of living out ways of seeing the world—these are what we study when we study religion, not a small or negligible thing. What is it, in particular, that as humanists we study in or about religion? It is not necessarily how people made things. It rather is why, or more really, how they told themselves the reason why. To be concrete, we may study the ancient temples of Egypt without studying the religion of ancient Egypt—until we want to know why people built those temples. The study of religion in a humanistic setting is the study of what people have made, have felt, and have been, because they were religious.

This description of what we study does not suggest what we hope to find out. Nor do I propose that a study is worth our while without regard to what we learn. On the contrary, not all information, not every datum, is of value or interest or even relevance. It is more important (to state matters in our obvious way) to know how to cure cancer than how to string a tennis racket. So the critical issue is what we hope to learn by understanding what religion is and means in the context of human knowledge. Still more, what do we learn from studying religion that we do not learn from systematically studying any other expression of humanity, not from the study of music, philosophy, or literature, for example.

The three most important results of humanistic study of religion deal with culture, history, and society. When we understand the religion of a group, we penetrate deep into its culture, its way of life. When we grasp the world-view of a people, we understand how it makes sense of events: how a group transforms this and that into history and destiny. When we accurately describe the way of life and world-view represented by culture and a sense for history, we grasp how a society hangs together, how religion serves to bond this one and that one into a coherent social group. So among the many things we learn about when we study a religion, the principal ones are, I believe, also critical to the interpretation of humanity at its irreducible and fundamental reality: culture, history, society.

The things people do every day because they are religious are not random. They are not mere customs and ceremonies, as people now say. Rather, they fit together into a whole and harmonious unit, a way of conducting life. Religion is what expresses, as the whole, the ethos of a group. In its power to encapsulate in immediate and concrete words, symbols or gestures, in laws and remissions from law, the deepest layers of culture and consciousness, religion reveals the whole as a whole. In an integrated and healthy system, there will be an interplay between (to use contemporary examples) the way we drive our cars and the way we fight our wars, the way we organize our economic life and the way we educate our children. That view of the interrelatedness of the constituents of culture presents no surprises. It is a commonplace, after all, to speak of consciousness and society, or of culture and conviction. Now, from the time of Marx and Weber, it has been equally commonplace to recognize that the religious convictions of a community express the community's deepest values. Hence, they shape and form its economic activity. Accordingly, it is not to claim too much when I allege that when we study religion we enter into the deepest layers of the culture of a group.

How we live out our lives in a common culture requires not merely deed but deliberation. For, as we all know, we not only do things but explain to ourselves what we do and why. For that purpose every group tells itself a story of who it is. In the nature of things, the story accounts for how the group has come into being and what is important in the things which have happened to the group. History, as distinct from narrative, comes into being as the explanation and expression of what has happened to the group. That explanation, it hardly needs saying, makes sense in particular of the way of life of the group, what it remembers and what it chooses to forget. History defines the events it takes as pardigmatic and those it treats as inconsequential. The formative power of religion in accounting for history hardly needs specification. If you want to understand how events are transformed into an intelligible account of reality, how the everyday becomes noteworthy, and how what I do is dictated by what I think I have been and must become, you had best study religion. The reason is that, for much of humanity now and most in the past, religion has given shape and meaning to events. That is why religion as a mode of interpreting and acting out history constitutes the second of the three principal foci of humanistic study of religion.

These two—way of life, world-view—demand yet a third focus. No system of living life and explaining it emerges from the pages of a book unless it enters into a social context, that is, forms, and is embodied by, society. To state matters simply: It is easy to explain how rites make sense of reason, and how ideas generate concrete action. For that purpose you write a book. No one need doubt that ethos and ethics are mutually explanatory. But to say of a system that it works and explain how, we have to point to the society which gives flesh and blood to the ethos and the ethics. When we turn to examine a society and ask how it holds its members together, defines its family-units and protects them, we turn to that third and critical component of the study of religion, namely, its power to bond society, to impart a shared vision and articulate a common cause. For it is religion which defines who is on the inside and who is on the outside: that is the beginning of the social group. The insider then is declared holy, the outsider, unclean; the insider practices supernatural powers, the outsider, magic; the insider speaks a language, the outsider says *bar bar bar*. Where shall we find the source of these ubiquitous distinctions, the secret of what makes a group see itself, but no one else, as a group, if not in religions? That is so not only in the premodern West. It is so in all of the modern world, whether the Middle East or Europe or North America today.

This rapid account of some part of what we hope to learn in the humanistic study of religion—of human visions of the divine—brings us to its counterpoint in humanistic study of Judaism, or, as stated in the beginning, Jewish studies as the humanities of the Jewish tradition. By the humanities of the Jewish tradition, by analogy to what already has been said, we mean the history, literature, philosophy, art, music, and other things Jews have made because they believed they are Israel, a holy people on earth. We mean these and also the towns and cities, the societies and systems of culture, all expressed and embodied in law, not a trivial matter. It is clear, I think, that nearly all of what the Jews have been and done throughout their history, they have been and done as Israel. That Jewish studies which systematically learn about these things therefore constitute a part of humanistic studies no longer requires argument. What demands attention, rather, is what we study when we see Jewish studies as the humanities of the Jews, and how we wish to study it. Let me rapidly spell out the humanistic questions to be raised in Jewish studies as a humanistic venture.

The questions to be addressed to the holy books of Judaism when they are read as "the humanities of the Jewish heritage" readily present themselves. What we want to know as humanistic scholars is about Judaism as a cultural system, Judaism as a mode of interpreting history, and Judaism as the means of bonding Jewish society. What I already have explained about what we principally study when we study religions and religion hardly demands extensive application to what we study when we engage in the humanistic study of Judaism. What we want to describe is how the various modes of human expression of Judaism fit together into a single and cogent culture. What we wish to analyze is how the things which happen to the Jews are transformed into history, made into a compelling statement of a unique destiny. That is, we want to know how Judaism constitutes a system for interpreting history and explaining why what happens is paradigmatic. When we have grasped the interplay between Judaism as a system of culture and Judaism as a mode of interpreting history, we have yet to complete the work. For at that point we turn to the critical issue of the interplay between Judaism and society, that is to say, Judaism as a means of bonding Jewish society, as the catalyst for the Jewish group. Once more we refer to the great exercise of Max Weber in asking about the interplay between economic behavior and religious belief. The larger question about how what I believe relates to my social situation is to be asked without in any way reducing belief to a function of sociology. These are three principal foci, then, for what we study when we pursue Jewish studies as the humanties of the Jewish tradition.

We face no considerable doubts in affirming that the humanistic study of humanity is congruent to the humanity that is studied. It requires no argument at all. But for the humanities as tools for Jewish learning, there are formidable obstacles to be considered. These may be stated very simply. What is important in Jewish studies, Judaism has always rightly held, is not what we learn about ourselves as a singular people. For Jewish studies study Torah, and, within that framework, what Jewish studies teach is not about what we have made, but what God has given to us, not about Israel, but what God wants of Israel. The humanities teach us what we are, perhaps also, what, in the vision of greater minds than ours, we may become and be. Jewish studies describe more than this. They tell also what we are supposed by God to be and to do. And it is the heart of Jewish studies—why they are holy, not merely interesting—that through Torah we learn about God's will for us. This is a very different thing from what we have done and been for ourselves. That is why the question of whether humanistic modes of learning are authentic and legitimate to the character and claim of Torah is an urgent question indeed.

To those who maintain that Jewish studies can be only for the sake of Torah, no argument will serve. By definition the holy books of Judaism may be read only in the holy places of Judaism, by Jews engaged in an act of worship and service of God through the study of Torah. When we evoke the criterion of the Jewish classics themselves, therefore, humanistic study of Judaism in no way may be deemed authentic to what is studied. And yet that cannot be the last word. For if we take up what is said about us as human beings in these same sources, we confront a stunning vision, a truly grand perspective upon ourselves. These sources do maintain, after all, that the issues of holiness devolve upon humanity: what we are, what we do, what we may become. When the Torah says, "Then God said, 'Let us make Adam in our image, after our likeness . . . ,'" it declares that to know humanity is to learn more about God. To study the history of Israel, the Jewish people, is to learn something about God's will. To interpret the norms for the holy life of Israel, the Jewish people, is to learn about the rules of sanctification. When the humanistic scholars of religions ask about Judaism as a way of shaping culture, interpreting history, and bonding society, how different are their questions from those who study the holy way of life, the meaning of the sacred history of Israel, and the modes of sanctification, through law, of the ongoing society of Israel? Once we understand that the sacred sciences address these questions, then we must concede that precisely the same questions emerge from the humanistic sciences. The humanistic approach to the study of religions, including Judaism, then, is authentic to the grandeur and high vision of what is studied: humanity at its most human, therefore at its most God-like.

From this brief account of a theory for Jewish studies as the humanities of the Jewish heritage, let me turn now to what I think a humanist would want to study. If I may point to what I believe the

HUMANITIES OF THE JEWISH HERITAGE 145

single most inviting area of contemporary Jewish studies, it is the study of Judaism, within the study of religion, in particular in the State of Israel. If, as I believe, this humanistic study of religions provides fresh perspectives and a new sense for the potentialities of the familiar, then we must ask, Where in the world do we find at hand the encounter and confrontation of great religions of humankind? It must be on a level plane, with ample space for movement and meeting. Those conditions are met when great and old religious traditions intersect in freedom and equality, in all their rich inner diversity, in all their distinctive inner cogency, in contrast to outsiders. Where may I find Judaism, Islam, and Christianity side by side, each represented by a range of authentic exemplars, if not in the State of Israel, and in Jerusalem in particular? It is startling to reflect that for the comparative study of living religions, the Jewish State, standing in humankind for the least of them all, should present the world with a living laboratory, a museum without walls, of the principal religions of the West. Yet in the study of religions, the least can be the greatest.

When we turn to the study of Judaism as a living religion, an available choice for salvation, we need hardly ask where to find the rich repertoire of potential and authentic choices, fully realized, amply exemplified. They are in the State of Israel. If the study of religion, including Judaism, permits us to investigate how culture takes shape, how events become history, and how society holds together, then where, if not in the State of Israel, shall we find the data for description, analysis and interpretation? Surely not where Judaism is a relic, as in a fair part of Europe and Africa, nor where, as in North America, it has become whatever people wish it to be, without the disciplines of learning and law.

And yet, while in the State of Israel Judaic religious tradition informs culture and bonds society, it also forms a point of contention and vigorous debate. Perhaps Judaism is too controversial to be studied. Perhaps opinions are held too fiercely and uncompromisingly. I cannot say. I know only that with negligible exceptions, not only are religions not studied in the universities of the Jewish State, as if religion were not a powerful force and a significant option for much of humankind. Judaism furthermore is allowed to be studied as anything but a religion. One may master the holy books in the old holy way or in new, still deeply convicted ways. One may live the holy way of life or any of its avatars and successors. But one may not study *about* these things in those academic humanistic ways in which, throughout the West, they are studied, analyzed, and interpreted. Perhaps the value of humanistic learning becomes clearest when, in a given set of data, it is not to be found. If that is so, we understand why the remarkable absence of a contemplative frame of mind, consciousness, and therefore, interest in competing views, and genuine sympathy for opposing, even rejected, opinions, characterizes discourse about, and within, Judaism in the State of Israel. So we see that where the "humanities of the Jewish heritage" are deemed a humanistic frame of reference, there the humanistic set of questions and attitudes of mind are prevented from making their contributions to civil discourse, which are reasoned reflection on deeply held convictions and a civilized society of the mind. And, as I said, where we witness the remarkable realization of Judaism and its rebirth is where we most miss the humanistic exploration of the extraordinary achievement of the Jews' sector of humanity, that is, Judaism.

When we consider, moreover, the tensions among living religions, the power of faith to generate hatred of the outsider, we must find urgent the study of religions within an academic, humanistic framework. For any path to understanding opens roads to peace. The purpose of studying religion in the setting of the humanities is to understand why people do what they do in the name of God. Since, in the West and Middle East, so much that they do is for God's sake, so much is done by holy writ and at the word of holy men, it is time we asked a fresh set of questions. For up to now, within the reservations of our respective faiths, we see the outsider as not only the enemy but the devil. That is to say, we do not understand, so we reject, condemn, avoid, declare crazy, unclean, unholy. We do not understand because we have no theory of the other, no way to make sense of the outsider, who lives by gibberish, so to speak.

Now there are two routes from one reservation to the next, one of good will, the other of learning. The former path serves few and leads nowhere beyond a wilderness of platitudes and clichés. As to the other—we do not know where it leads because it is the way not yet taken. And yet the way of learning is to be described. I mean a path paved not with facts—one group believes this, the other eats that, the third marks the moon's rise. It is a path not paved at all, marked out, rather, by guideposts. These are three: description, analysis, interpretation. Description puts facts together into meaningful structures, systems in which the facts make sense to someone, if not to all. Analysis makes sense of facts in yet another way. I mean, not only as they fall together to the one inside, but also, how they make a different sort of sense to the observer. When we ask what sort of things people believe, and how what they do expresses what they believe, we describe in a coherent way. We turn facts into intelligible knowledge,

HUMANITIES OF THE JEWISH HERITAGE

exemplifications of generally accessible propositions. When, further, we take the system, now described, and ask analytical questions about how it functions within a larger social and political ecology, we find ourselves engaged in a labor of interpretation. To describe, to analyze—these prepare the way for the hardest work, interpretation, the exercise of taste and experienced judgment. We interpret religions when we see them whole and at work. That perspective—to see the whole whole, so to speak—is made possible when we see the parts as segments of a larger context, when we ask questions of comparison. These are important, because they allow us to contrast one world with some other, to discover what is unlike because it stands upon a common continuum in humanity, to uncover what is common through scrutiny of what is not.

For in the end we shall understand the other best when we see the choices before us all and understand that we do make choices, because we have freedom to choose. To interpret religions we mean to grasp the choices people make, to do some thing rather than some other, to eat this, not that, to live within some ethos, rather than some other. To state matters simply, to describe religions, we must become historians. To analyze religions, we must become sociologists, for the social side to things, and philosophers, for the intellectual side. To interpret religions, we must turn ourselves into anthropologists of a certain sort, I mean, with a small *a*, merely students of humanity, of ourselves. The work of interpretation, indeed, demands all of the gifts of the entire range of the humanities.

In all the world religions are studied. But it is mainly in America that *religion*, too, is studied. Everywhere, East and West, religions and their surrogates are cultivated—indeed treated quite rightly as the binding of society, the core of culture, the mode of finding one's place in time and space and history, the condition of consciousness. But where societies are diverse, religions and their surrogates prove divisive. In America, from World War II onward, our common task has been to uncover the sources of unity among a people not only diverse but now at last disposed to honor difference. But how are we to live together in difference—this has been our national quest, our American dilemma. It is a country of difference from the color of our people's skins to the shape of their noses. There are no commonalities but language and loyalty, on the one side, and a fear of commonality, of absorption into an undifferentiated mass, on the other. Now that was the context in which the humanistic study of religions was born. That is the frame within which we who propose to describe, analyze, and interpret Judaism do our work.

Up to now I have treated as self-evident the importance of the humanistic study of religions. Let me now spell out why I think this approach to religion and to the study of Judaism is an urgent task for the society of Judaism. To understand the promise of the humanistic study of Judaism, we must make sense of why, to begin with, humanists turned to religion. Let me therefore explain briefly, in just a few sentences, the history of the humanistic study of religions, including Judaism, in America. Before World War II, religions were studied only for theological purposes, that is, as divine sciences. Afterward there was a sincere effort to study other religions than one's own. This represented the beginning of the humanistic study of religions. There have been three main stages. First, we organized departments of religious studies in which Catholic priests taught mainly Catholics about Catholicism, rabbis taught Jews about Judaism, and Buddhist holy men taught everybody else. Legitimate classroom discourse involved rabbis interrogating Jewish students about why they were atheists. There was not a department of religion; there were only diverse religions, each a specimen of itself alone. We now look back on that period's departments and call them zoos: each species in its cage. In the second stage, we tried to teach several distinct religious traditions in a single context, so we organized courses in Catholicism, Protestantism, and Judaism. There was, further, a pretense of comparison, but mainly it consisted of much good will and little shared comprehension. We had not left the zoo; we had merely enlarged the cages.

Now, at the present stage, as is clear, our effort is to find a common program of questions to address to diverse religions, that is, to ask questions of the humanities. Our work is to treat the various religious traditions as exemplary. Given religions, at a given point in their history and society, may offer interesting data to exemplify a phenomenon of religion important beyond themselves. What is important only for itself teaches mere facts. What is important beyond itself, what supplies an *e.g.*, so to speak, is what we seek for religion in the several religious traditions before us.

That is why I pointed to the power of Judaism to exemplify how a religious tradition informs culture, interprets history, and shapes society. That, further, is the reason that the State of Israel constitutes one of the great unexplored territories for the humanistic study of religions. At the same time, I repeat, when this work makes its contribution, the result is to overcome polemic and to introduce a measure of understanding and mutual comprehension. For in the end, when we exemplify, we address a world beyond ourselves. We reach out to the other and see ourselves in the stranger, and the stranger in ourselves. That is the task before us.

So I argue that, when we approach the sacred and revealed texts of Torah as the humanities of the Jewish tradition, we ask a fresh set of questions. We address texts with the power to speak to many sorts of questions. We seek to state what we think is human and worth sharing out of the experience of the Jewish people, as distinct from what is divine and definitive of our distinctive being. For we are both human, exemplifications of humanity, and also Israel, distinctive and distinct within humanity. Our humanness and distinctiveness are wholly bonded within what we call, on the one side, Torah, but also our version of the humanities, on the other. Now it is this humanistic dimension of Jewish studies which requires attention, just as the humanistic issues inhering in Islam and Christianity do, in the humanistic study of religions.

The reason is that when we describe, analyze, and interpret religions, we come to a better understanding of that protean force, religion, within this world. In that way we make better sense not of ourselves alone but of others. The motive of understanding religions is to overcome that dislike of the unlike which makes for hatred and war. But how are we to learn to describe, analyze, and interpret what is different from ourselves? In the humanistic study of religions, we seek those intellectually sound methods for description, analysis, and interpretation which permit us to see the other in ourselves, and ourselves in the other, all examples of a shared existence. When the humanistic study of religions succeeds, the alien seems less strange. Then too, the self seems more strange. The alien is within. Where we are most at home, there we are mostly strangers. It is when we understand that, in the work of learning, we remain perpetually outsiders in our own richly complex, astonishing traditions, strangers where we feel most at home, that the humanistic study of religions begins.

APPENDIX
Clearing Away Some More Debris: Defining the Humanities

Harold Cannon
National Endowment for the Humanities

I take my point of departure from Jacob Neusner's article,[1] and must differ with him at the outset about the definition of "definition." I define "definition" as the act of limiting in words so effectively as to pin down the meaning of a concept without chance of movement and hence of change. The Romans believed they were describing boundaries around a concept when they defined it, and the Greeks thought of the horizon as an extreme physical limitation. My field is defined by these three hedges and that dry stone wall, said the ancient farmer.

The Congressional definition (or "definition") cited in this article states that "the term humanities includes, but is not limited to, the study of the following. . . . " and then a catalogue follows. Since there are no limitations here, there is no definition. To be a definition, this paragraph should tell us what may or may not be excluded.[2] In its present form, it lacks that specificity. It is worth noting, too, inclusions we do have suggest powerful overlapping with the National Science Foundation (linguistics, archaeology, e.g.) and with the National Endowment for the Arts ("the history, criticism, theory, and practice of the arts"[3]). I think this process should begin by posing the question of a prerequisite: what study must underlie work in the humanities to authenticate that style? In the sciences, the necessary underpining seems to be mathematics; a scientist without mathematical skills can scarcely be conceived. The equivalent for the humanities is not single field but a combination of history, language, and literature that enables thought to be expressed in language appropriate to intellectual context and historical connotation. I sense a distinction here between England

---

[1] Pp. 3–12.
[2] It is scarcely informative to say, "My field includes, but is not limited to, this patch of ground between us and the river."
[3] The words "and practice" were recently excised from the law.

and the United States: I think the English common ground is more literary and the American more historical—an interesting commentary on the cultural needs of the older and the younger society!

I deduce this "common ground" theory from eight years' observation of the Endowment's review processes. In the absence of any definition of the humanities in this agency's Congressional mandate, every application must demonstrate its humanistic credentials as a passport. Distinguishing the elect, therefore, is fodder for panels, and I have noticed that they rely heavily on historical-cum-literary touchstones. They look for something called "depth" or "context" and for some assessment of the aesthetic value of the word: one or the other will suffice, but the most likely candidates display both—like an allowable passport with a pertinent visa stamped into it.

If you work back from this analysis of actual experience (and how can experience fall to be actual?) with the decision-making process, you have some structure for a definition. The humanities must be those areas of study that connote historical and literary concerns. But, since that excludes philosophy and does not allow for the purely historical or purely literary, we should try something like this: the humanities are the studies that connote either historical, literary, or philosophical concerns.

The first thing to notice about this draft definition is that it includes all the other bits and pieces in the Congressional catalogue. Language is essential to literature, as are some aspects of linguistics; jurisprudence combines all three prime elements at its best; archaeology is surely historical; comparative religion is historical and philosophical; ethics is a branch of philosophy; all aspects of the arts other than their practice are included; and we have a clearer notion of social science prospects with this formula in mind, since it tells us what is meant by "humanistic content" and "humanistic methods."

I would like to submit also the radical notion that the study of the humanities is not a matter of choice but necessary function of the human condition. One may choose to study nuclear physics or to compose a string quartet, but the study of history is, simply, not to be avoided by any of us. Perhaps "study" is too strong a word; "attention" might be more accurate. Memory was the mother of the muses, the Greeks believed, and history is a development of human memory. We are all walking archives of our own experience, and we know something of our parents', relatives' and friends' histories too. This attention to history is a long way from the profession of historian, and the emphasis on it may vary from slight to extreme. But I submit that it is there, even in an illiterate, and that a similar argument could be made for language/literature, and even for philosophy.

APPENDIX 153

Encouraging more attention of this sort among nonprofessionals (if you will) is a very important part of the Endowment's mandate. It is there, I believe because of the idea that the life both of individuals and of societies is thereby enhanced. The arguments brought forward to support this thesis range from developing an electorate that will support an enlightened foreign policy to maintaining a society that cares about Gadsby's Tavern and the Willard Hotel. It may be too utopian to suggest it as a crime-fighter, but I would pit the humanities, with their stress on individual merit, against communism any day!

Far too often, however, the nonprofessionals are invited to sit tamely as an audience to witness a professional engaging in the humanities. This may be entertaining, and it may have connections with the humanities, but such audiences are not participating in the humanities during this exercise. There is nothing passive about the humanities; essentially, they are the argumentative fields, and none every enjoyed a one-sided argument. That is why I do not believe that the Jefferson lecture is an event in the humanities; the discussions and arguments that succeed the lecture—*there* is the action of the humanities.

For centuries, the priesthood has kept these rites apart; "odi profanum vulgus et arceo," said the Roman poet Horace. Part of the Endowment's job is to destroy those ancient barriers, deny certification, and encourage everyone to talk as loudly and as often as they wish about human record, notions, and values.

What it is all about is a sense of mastery; that has some of the quality of illusion but, even amid life's physical uncertainties, there are areas that can be brought under intellectual control. And that is both satisfying and exciting. Anyone who has taught knows how bewildered the young can be. Ignorance is not bliss but a continual torture. To know something for sure, and to know how to do something effectively and efficiently—that is the point to which the young aspire, that is what education is about. The Endowment is in the teaching business; they ask us for bread, and we will not give them stones.

INDEX
To Biblical and Talmudic References

BIBLE

I Corinthians	
8:5	102
II Corinthians	
4:4	102
Genesis	
1:1–2:4a	123, 127

MISHNAH

Menahot	
1:1–4:5	129
Ohalot	
9:1–14	125
Kelim	
17:11	128
Shebiit	
6:1–6	126
Zebahim	
1:1–4:6	129

GENERAL INDEX

Agriculture, economics in Ancient Judaism, 116-35
American Academy for Jewish Research, 60
American Academy of Religion, 30
American Council of Learned Societies, 46
American Judaism, study of, 76-78
Ancient Judaism, economics in, 116-35; order and stability, 131-35; religion and society, 113-35
Application of the humanities, 5-6, 8-11, 15, 19
Appointed times, economics in Ancient Judaism, 116-24
'Aqiba, Scripture and law, 109-10, 112
Ashly, Gardner, 59
Association for Jewish Studies, 60

Barcroft, John H., defining humanities, 9-10, 12
Baron, Salo W., 55
Bellah, R., 31
Bendix, Reinhard, 113, 115, 135
Ben Gurion, David and King David, comparisons, 93
Berman, Ronald, 10n
Biography and Talmudic "Lives," 107-12
Boyce, Mary, 96
Brandeis University and Jewish learning, 57, 63
Brown University, higher Jewish learning, 56, 61
Buddhism, study of, 148

Cannon, Harold, defining humanities, 151-53
Catholicism, humanities and study of religions, 148
Central Conference of American Rabbis, 58
Cherniss, Harold, 115
Christianity, cultural philosophies, 101-5; and Judaic study, 81-82; similarity of doctrines, 96-97
Commentary in Judaic study, 84
Comparison and analysis of religions, 91-100
Constituency of humanities, 13-22; responsibilities of higher Jewish learning, 55-66; underserved constituencies and National Endowment for the Humanities, 39

Contemporary life and religious study, 23-38
Cultures, cultural characteristics and religious traditions, 93-100; Judaism and cultural system, 139-49; philosophies of religions, 101-5; and religious studies, 27-38

Daily living, exposure to humanities, 14-16
Damages, religion and society in Ancient Judaism, 118-19
Defining humanities, Harold Cannon, defining, 151-53; problems of, 3-22
Democracy and its demands on humanities, 7-8
Differentiation and analysis of religions, 91-100
Disciplines, interdependence with religious studies, 28-38; relevance of humanities to personal experience, 17-18
Diversity in Judaism, 91-100
Douglas, M., 31
Dropsie University, higher Jewish learning, 56-58, 63-66
Duffey, Joseph, 10n
Durkheim, E., 27-31

Economics, characteristics and religious traditions, 93-100; Mishnah and social setting, 116-24
Education, Office of, defining humanities, 9-10, 12
Eliezer, Scripture and law, 108-9
Eliezer b. Hyrcanus, rabbinic biography and Talmudic "Lives," 108
Essene community, Judaism of, 91
Ethics and religious studies, 27-38
Experience, relevance of humanities to personal experience, 17-18
Expression, defining humanistic expression, 6, 8, 10, 16
Exxon Education Foundation, 39

Faddism and sloganeering in religious studies, 30-31
Federation Reports, 4
Feldman, Louis H., 104-5
Foreign language, need in religious studies, 32-38
Freud, Sigmund, 27

Gamaliel, Scripture and law, 108-9
Geertz, C., 31
Geographic characteristics and religious traditions, 93-100
Goldenberg, David, 66
Goodenough, Erwin, 96-97

Hebrew Union College Annual, 59
Hebrew Union College-Jewish Institute of Religion, 58-59
Hellenism, cultural philosophies, 101-5

INDEX 159

Hengel, Martin, 104-5
Historical characteristics and religious traditions, 93-100
History of Judaism, courses in, 72-76
"Holocaust" and Jewish learning, 61-62
Humanistic expression, defining of, 6, 8, 10, 16
Humanistic learning, daily exposure to humanities, 14-16
Humanities, Harold Cannon defining, 151-53; legally defined, 3-4, 6, 9; problems in defining, 3-22; study engendering unity, 139-49; versus communism, 153
Humanity, study of man as humanities, 13-22

Ishmael, Scripture and law, 108-9
Islam, similarity of doctrines, 96-97
"Israel," comparison and differentiation, 95

Jewish heritage and Jewish learning, 139-49
Jewish humanities, higher Jewish learning, responsibilities of, 55-56; public programs, 49-52
Jewish learning, Jewish heritage, 139-49; Jewish theological study, 62; Judaism study courses, 67-82; responsibilities of, 55-66
Jewish Theological Seminary of America and Jewish learning, 58-59
Joshua, Scripture and law, 109-10
Judaic study, American Judaism, 76-78; Christianity, value in study of, 81-82; commentary, importance of, 84; contemporary expressions, 74-76; course syllabus, 70-81; history of Judaism, 72-76; Jewish learning, 83-87; Judaism in late antiquity, 79-81; motion pictures in religious study, 71-72; reading programs, 72-91; Zionism, 78-79
Judaism, Ancient Judaism, religion and society, 113-35; availability of learning, 49-52; cultural philosophies, 101-5; cultural system, 139-49; diversity of, 91-100; humanistic studies and unity, 139-49; humanities and study of religions, 148; Jewish learning, 83-87; Scripture and law, 110, 112; similarity of doctrines, 96-97; study courses, 67-82: *see also* Ancient Judaism, Judaic study

Language, communality of in religious traditions, 94-95, 98; complicating definition of humanities, 8-9; need for foreign language in religious studies, 32-38
Lieberman, Saul, 103
List-making to define humanities, 4-7, 10-11, 13-22
Literature, American Jewish literature and Jewish learning, 57, 62; Mishna, methods of thought, 124-31
Lyman, Richard, 4, 7

Maimonides and Judaism, 91
Man, study of, as humanities, 13–22
Meir, Scripture and law, 110, 112
Mishnah, literary traits, 124–31; order and stability, 131–35; religion and society in Ancient Judaism, 113–35; social setting, 116–24
Motion pictures in religious studies, 71–72, 75, 79
Motz, Julie, 43
Muslims, similarity of doctrines, 96–97

National Council on the Humanities, 37: *see also* National Endowment for the Humanities
National cultural policy and National Endowment for the Humanities, 39–44
National Endowment for the Arts, 151
National Endowment for the Humanities, 37; decision making, 39–44; defining humanities, 3–4, 6, 9, 14–15, 19; functions and grants, 39–44; Jewish humanities and public programs, 49–52; national cultural policy, 39–44; objectives, 15; open meetings, 45–47; policy, 45–52; procedures, 39–44; public business and open meetings, 45–47; yardsticks, 39–44
National Foundation on the Arts and Humanities Act of 1965, humanities legally defined, 3–4, 6, 9
National Humanities Center in North Carolina, 64
National Meeting of State Humanities Programs, 4
National Science Foundation, 151

Office of Education, 9–10, 12
Open meetings of National Endowment for the Humanities, 45–47

Parallels in religious study, problems of comparison, 95–97
Personal experience, relevance of humanities to, 17–18
Political behavior and religious convictions, 28
Political characteristics and religious traditions, 93–100
Protestantism, humanities and study of religions, 148; Protestant culture, 29–30
Public business and open meetings of National Endowment for the Humanities, 45–47
Public responsibilities for humanities, 14–22
Purities, religion and society in Ancient Judaism, 116–17
Purpose of humanities, statement as definition, 3–12

Qumran community, Judaism of, 91

Rabbinic biography and Talmudic "Lives," 107–12
Rabbinical Assembly and Jewish learning, 58–59
Rabbis, scribes becoming, 119–20
Religion, Ancient Judaism and society, 113–35; humanistic study of, 23–38

INDEX 161

Religious study, Judaic courses, 67–82; motion pictures in, 71–72; universality of, 23–38
Religious traditions, characteristics of, 93–110
Right to know, National Endowment for the Humanities and open meetings, 45–47
Rockefeller Foundation, 4

Sabbateans, Judaism of, 92
Sanctification, systems of, 92–93
Scholarly grants, National Endowment for the Humanities, procedures, 39–44
Scholarship, public responsibilities of humanities, 14–22
Scribes-become-rabbis, Ancient Judaism, 119–20
Scripture, as common language, 95; law and Talmudic literature, 107–12
Simeon, Scripture and law, 110
Sloganeering and faddism in religious studies, 30–31
Smith, Morton, comparison and differentiation in religious study, 9, 95–96; cultural philosophies of religions, 102–4
Social behavior and religious convictions, 28
Social characteristics and religious traditions, 93–100
Society, Ancient Judaism and religion, 113–35; and Mishnah, 116–24
Sociology and religious studies, 29
Symbolism defining humanities, 4

Talmudic literature, Scripture and law, 107–12
Tarfon, Scripture and law, 108–10

Unity, study of humanities engendering, 139–49

Weber, Max, 27, 31, 113–15, 134–35, 141, 143
Wolfson, H. A., 55
Women, cultures recognizing status of, 96–98; religion and society in Ancient Judaism, 118–19

Yosé, Scripture and law, 110

Zionism, Jewish learning, 57; in Judaic study, 78–79
Zoroaster, similarity of doctrines, 96–97